CONTENTS

SUNDAY AFTERNOONS AND OTHER TIMES REMEMBERED

SUNDAY AFTERNOONS AND OTHER TIMES REMEMBERED

A Memoir

BEN EWELL

SPARKPRESS

Published by SparkPress, a BookSparks imprint,
A division of SparkPoint Studio, LLC
Phoenix, Arizona, USA, 85007
www.gosparkpress.com

Published 2022
Printed in the United States of America

Print ISBN: 978-1-68463-141-4
E-ISBN: 978-1-68463-142-1
Library of Congress Control Number: 2021925478

Formatting by Katherine Lloyd/The DESK

For Mom and Dad
(Forever on my mind)

For Dale, Glee, Tiffany, Betty, and Dan
(My past)

For Suzy, Harrison, John John, Tucker,
Austin, and Brice
(My future)

Chapter 1

MURDER ON EASTER SUNDAY

Moving slowly around the cemetery's sweeping circular drive surrounded on both sides by freshly mowed grass and bright spring flowers tended by a single gardener, our car slowed to a gentle stop. The April sky that Saturday morning looked unusually blue, with puffy white clouds of the kind I often saw in Ohio but seldom in Fresno.

As I opened the car door, I could hear the birds of spring chirp and sing to each other in a symphony of nature. Three identical wooden coffins came into view resting upon waist-high stands under a green canopy of tall pine trees. A row of white folding chairs had been placed on the grass in front of the coffins. My thoughts returned to those peaceful days on our Ohio farm many years before: Saturday mornings working side by side with my brothers in hot, humid, thick, almost unbreathable air, as we all helped Dad, and again in subzero winter weather, cutting and chopping wood for our furnace, each bundled against the cold; and Sundays, a day of rest and family, adhering to Dad's rule of no work on the seventh day. How I missed those days now.

I stepped out of the funeral home limousine first and helped Dad, now eighty-five, out of his seat as two other cars pulled up and parked behind us. A lot, too much, had happened to our family in the six days before that Saturday morning. My brothers and I had learned that our eldest brother, Dale, his wife, Glee, and their daughter, Tiffany, had been shot and killed in their home on Easter Sunday afternoon.

I could not make my mind believe these stark wooden coffins contained three family members who had been murdered in their home, by whom or for what reason we did not know. The small family burial taking place that morning had been intentionally private with no public announcement of time or location.

Dad and my sister Betty had just flown in together from Ohio. Betty sat beside Dad in front of the coffins on one side. I sat next to Dad on the other side with my fiancée, Suzy Harris, along with my brothers, Richard and Dan, and Dan's wife, Susan. My now deceased sister-in-law Glee's mother, "Big Glee" Mitchell, her caretaker, and my nephew Dana sat by themselves at the end of the row. The handful of us spoke only a little to each other. What could any of us have said that morning?

I kept my sunglasses on at the cemetery to shield my eyes from the warming morning sun and to hide my persistent tears. I don't recall the minister's brief remarks that morning at the cemetery, only Dad's remark at the end of the service, as he choked back tears and said, "What a waste of life."

When the brief service ended, I rose and walked to the three caskets, stopping briefly to touch each of them as I passed by. The image of each of the three family members came to me as I walked back to the limousine. My brother Dale was a six-foot, three-inch successful businessman who I thought fit the cliché of tall, dark haired, and handsome. He was direct and to the point but with never a harsh word for me, and he always had time to listen and help his younger brother. Glee, my sister-in-law, was a Phi Beta Kappa graduate of the University of Arizona and the Thunderbird

2

School of Foreign Trade, a former CIA agent, and later a high school Spanish language teacher who liked books, politics, and community service. I could relate to all three of her interests. I loved to discuss the latest world happenings with her and read the books she gave me. Then I thought of my niece Tiffany, Dale and Glee's beautiful blonde, blue-eyed, twenty-four-year-old daughter. She was quiet, soft-spoken, and outwardly timid, even after graduating from a small college in Oregon. She had been taking graduate courses and was ready to start a career. She never had a bad word to say about anyone or anything.

About three hours later at the First Congregational Church on Van Ness Boulevard in Fresno, a public funeral service took place. The smell of the flower arrangements at the front of the sanctuary, especially the lilies, made me nauseous. My body tensed up upon seeing and greeting others. Every day since the sheriff had arrived at the crime scene, the local newspaper had run a large, front-page headline and story about our family. Some attendees at the funeral seemed to stare at us, while others didn't make eye contact—or was I just imagining it? *Look, there are the Ewells,* I thought they must be saying. "I would rather be anywhere else," I said, though only to myself, and under my breath.

My inability to understand this tragedy affected me more at first than the sadness I would feel later. There were no goodbyes to our family members before their deaths nor even a chance to view them in a funeral home visitation setting. The funeral home representative told us the caskets would remain closed because of the condition of the bodies.

On the previous Tuesday morning, April 21, 1992, my secretary, Toni Breadmont, caught my attention as I walked into my office at the Brighton Crest Golf Course in the foothills near Fresno.

"Ed Hunt, the district attorney, is calling," she said. I had known Ed for years. We first became friends when he was just beginning to be active in politics, and I was the Young Republican chairman.

"You better take the call; he says it's important," Toni reminded me.

As soon as I pushed the blinking light on the phone, I recognized Ed's Alabama twang.

"Ben, it's me, Ed. Are you sitting down?"

"No, why, what's going on?" I asked. (I thought, *That's what people say when they're going to deliver bad news.*) To brace myself, I placed my hand on the corner of Toni's desk.

Ed said in a soft but clear voice, "Ben, I hate to be the one to tell you this, but has anyone talked to you today about your family?"

"No, nobody." I could feel my body stiffen at the mention of the word *family* from the DA, wondering which family he was talking about.

"Well," he said, "your brother Dale, his wife, Glee, and your niece have all been shot and killed in their home."

I was silent as he continued, just trying to absorb the unthinkable.

"The bodies are still at the house," he said, and then stopped talking.

"Ed, what happened?" I managed to ask, almost in a whisper, sounding desperate.

"I can't talk right now," he said. "Take down my home number and call me tonight." I grabbed a pen and tore off a piece of scrap paper to write on.

"Are you ready? Here's the number." He went on speaking in short, fast phrases and then hung up. I called Ed that night at his home. When he got on the phone he said, "I can't really talk about it, but we're looking at folks around the dinner table." I didn't know what he meant, and he didn't explain.

Feeling light-headed, I slumped into a chair next to Toni's

desk. My eyes filled with tears. *How could this be?* My hand holding the phone receiver began to shake, and I couldn't get it back into the phone cradle. Clearing my throat, I blurted out to Toni, "They're all dead; they've been killed."

"Who's dead?" she asked.

"Dale, Glee, Tiffany," I whispered. "I need to call Dan. I need to tell him what happened."

"I think you need to wait and tell Dan in person," Toni replied.

Maybe she was right. My brother Dan had had two minor heart attacks years before, and this news might just be too much for him. Calling Dan's secretary, Carol McDougal, Toni told her what we had learned from the district attorney and said not to tell Dan but to drive over and meet us at his house.

"We should go there now," Toni said. "Let me drive your car, and you can ride with me. I'll just leave my car here."

I started to feel wobbly and fainter, and tears came to my eyes and ran down my cheeks. I put on my sunglasses and walked out of the office, strangely wondering what others in the office might think about my crying. From my early childhood days on our Ohio farm, I'd learned that boys and certainly men, including my brothers and me, didn't really show emotion, cry, or hug people, and the trait had mostly stayed with me.

When we arrived at Dan's Fresno home, he walked out to the driveway to meet us, saying Carol had already told him.

"Richard's on his way back to Fresno from the Bay Area. He should be here anytime now," Dan said. Richard, who now lived in Fresno, had been away on business.

Instead of calling Dad in Ohio, I thought I should first call my sister, Betty, who lived in Ashland, about forty miles from Dad's place. Betty had gone to visit Dad almost every weekend since Mom died. She took care of his house and cooked meals for him.

I reached Betty at her Ashland University office. She listened without comment as I told her what had happened to Dale, Glee, and Tiffany. She didn't ask for any details. Betty had suffered in her own life with an alcoholic husband, a son who disappeared for years without a trace, and long-standing tensions with our mom. She had always had a complete disdain for California and what happened there. She replied in what I knew to be her usual controlled voice and expression, brought on by years of living with her own problems.

"I need to drive over and tell Dad in person. I don't want to do this over the phone," she said. "I'll wait to tell him later tonight, and I'll stay with him. I don't want him to be alone afterward."

I told her we all appreciated her help with Dad and thought she was doing the right thing by telling him in person.

Dan, still standing in his driveway, said, "I can't believe it. I just talked to Dale on Good Friday. He came by to look at his lot next door." The lot was where he and Glee intended to build their new home. They already had a model made of their future home on the San Joaquin River bluff across the fence from Dan. Dale had mentioned to Dan that he had an appointment that day at Joe's Barber Shop to get a haircut before he left town to spend Easter weekend with his family at our beach house.

I said to Dan, "Glee left a message on my home answering machine thanking me for switching weekends so she and Dale could spend Easter at the beach house."

Dale had come up with the idea of building a house on the beach at the water's edge in Pajaro Dunes, a resort development just south of Santa Cruz. I was just getting out of law school at the time. He oversaw the design and construction of the two-story house on the sand with the water of Monterey Bay about fifty feet away. It had four bedrooms, three baths, and plenty of room for our entire family. His plan for the beach house had the four

6

brothers owning it in equal shares. When it was completed, Dale's wife, Glee, set up a schedule for all of us to use the house equally each year, rotating the times between each of the four brothers and their families. Each of us had use of the home one week per month, and we shared holidays. Still single and just getting started practicing law, I told Dale I wouldn't be able to put up my quarter of the cost and become an equal partner.

Dale said, "Don't worry, Ben. I'll give you the money, and you can pay me back sometime later," which I did.

Over the years we had great times at the house with family get-togethers when Mom and Dad visited, and other times with friends. My fondest memories of the beach at Pajaro Dunes were from early in the days when my two sons, Brice and Austin, were young. We would walk on the long, wide beach looking for sand dollars, hoping to find the little creatures still alive and intact, not yet having been pecked apart by sandpipers. We often came upon remnants of beach bonfires from the previous night that had since burned out, like the ones we started almost every night ourselves. I spent many weekends at the beach house over the years, often just walking along the water's edge, looking for shells and thinking of both the difference and likeness to the Ohio farm. Although at opposite ends of the country, both places had a serene, peaceful feel. Even though initially we may see places as completely differ-ent from where we live or work, often after further observation, many if not most things have some common thread that we will eventually recognize and appreciate.

Easter of 1992 would have been my turn to use the Pajaro Dunes house, but a few weeks earlier, Glee had called and asked if we could trade so she could use the house on Easter. I told her it would not be a problem.

Not long after I arrived at Dan's home, he had a call from the Fresno County Sheriff's Office on his unlisted home phone number. The caller asked Dan to come downtown with his brothers to meet with a detective there.

"Before I go downtown, I need to go by school and get my boys," I told Dan. Thoughts raced through my head. *What was happening? Three family members killed; could there be more? Who was behind this? Were other family members targets? Am I next?* I didn't know. The superior court had awarded me custody of my two sons in the divorce proceedings from my first wife, and she had visitation every other weekend. I had received numerous threats from my ex-wife's male friends at the time, some implied and others direct. I never took them too seriously, but now I was afraid there might be a connection.

Arriving at Tenaya Middle School, I told the receptionist we had a family emergency and I needed to pick up my son Austin. Checking the roster, she said he was on a class trip and wouldn't be back until after lunch. I left Tenaya and drove over to Malloch Elementary School, to pick up ten-year-old Brice. The Malloch school kids were on lunch break, and the office assistant said I could find him on the playground. As I walked across the playground toward a group of screaming, laughing kids, I saw Brice. I thought, *Don't these kids know what I'm going through right now? No, of course they don't.*

Brice ran up to me and asked, "Dad, why are you here?"

I leaned down to talk to him. "Something has happened to Uncle Dale and Aunt Glee. Just come with me; we can talk more about it later."

Brice, in his short ten years of life, had already been through a lot of trauma resulting from the divorce and the child custody hearings that followed. As could be expected, he seemed confused by what I said. He grew silent and just stared ahead.

I drove back to Tenaya Middle School and found that Austin had returned from the field trip. I repeated what I'd said to Brice.

"Something has happened to Uncle Dale and Aunt Glee." Before he got the words "What happened?" out, I said, "Just come with me, and we can talk later."

I dropped both boys off at my home to stay with my fiancée, Suzy, and drove back to Dan's place. I told the boys only that something had happened to their aunt and uncle, and we were trying to find out more. When they asked what had happened, I assured them I would talk to them later about it. I'm sure they noticed my distress, though I tried to cover it up.

When we arrived at the sheriff's office, Dan, Richard, and I introduced ourselves to the receptionist through a hole at the bottom of what looked like a bulletproof glass window.

She turned and said something to people behind her, presumably that we had arrived.

The sheriff's building had a stark, colorless lobby and a wall hung with pictures of former Fresno County sheriffs and the dates they served, including the current sheriff, Steve Magarian. On another wall hung several "WANTED" posters. A man came out of a side door and motioned for us to follow him. We walked behind him down a dimly lit hallway to a small room consisting of a few metal chairs and a metal desk. The officer behind the desk stood and introduced himself, but because I was so stressed, I didn't catch his name.

"Sit down. I have something to tell you about your brother and his family," he said.

I cleared my throat, interrupting him.

"We know about the killings," I said abruptly.

"How?" he asked, seeming agitated. "How'd ya find out?"

"From Ed Hunt. He's a friend, and he called me."

"Well, he shouldn't have," he replied.

I thought, *What difference does that make?* I later learned that every family member is an initial suspect in a crime involving other members of the family, and a family member's first physical and emotional reaction to hearing the news of a crime can be an important factor in the investigation.

The detective continued, "What about your brother Dale and his family? What can you tell me?"

Dan spoke up saying that Dale owned Western Piper Sales, a Fresno aircraft dealership, along with several orange and pistachio orchards in the Fresno and Madera area. Dan continued that Dale's wife, Glee, an only child, had grown up in Oklahoma. Glee's grandfather, a country doctor, had acquired considerable Oklahoma oil and gas properties in exchange for medical bills for services he rendered to folks who couldn't pay cash.

"Glee used to be in the CIA," I volunteered abruptly. "I still have the camel saddle she sent me from Egypt."

"What about their kids?" he inquired, not seeming interested in the CIA or camel saddle information.

Dan said, "Tiffany, their daughter, is blonde, blue-eyed, in her twenties, and really quiet."

I told him, "They have one boy, Dana."

"What's he like?" asked the detective.

Dan again spoke up. "He's attending the University of Santa Clara. When we do see him, he's usually on a computer working on something, doesn't really hang out with his cousins. Let's just say, he seems a little different. He doesn't seem to act or talk like a teenager with the usual interest in sports or girls. He wants to talk about business and usually asks me about the real estate deals I'm working on." I thought that Dan's description of Dana seemed about right.

"Well, okay," the detective said. "That's it for now. We'll be in touch," he finished, getting up from behind the metal desk to show us the door.

▶ THE FUNERAL

We drove back to Dan's house after the sheriff's interview discussing funeral arrangements along the way. I offered to call Dan Whitehurst, a friend, fellow lawyer, and former mayor of Fresno. Dan and his family had been involved for years in some manner with Whitehurst Funeral Chapel, which bore their name. I recalled a conversation he and I had one time over lunch about the funeral business. His comments went through my mind again that day.

"Ben, it's no different than any other business," he said. "We call preparation of a body for burial a 'case,' and we handle hundreds of cases every year."

I listened to him, not convinced it was that simple or unemotional.

When I reached Whitehurst on the phone and explained why I was calling, he said, "Ben, I'd like to help out, but we sold the family business some time ago, and they just kept our name. Here's the number you should call."

After calling, I explained our situation and asked what we should do. The receptionist said, "We'll send someone out tomorrow night at seven. Where should we meet you?"

I gave her Dan's home address.

Later that night, after I was sure Betty had already told Dad, I called him in Ohio. He repeated what Betty had said in soft, almost inaudible words.

"Betty and I are coming out there," Dad said. His voice started to quiver, and I could tell then he was on the verge of crying.

I said, "Okay," which was my only response. I wanted to comfort him and help him, but I couldn't. He was three thousand miles away. I could see him only in my mind and my thoughts.

An old black-and-white photo came to mind of a proud farm dad with his arm around his small son Dale next to a lamb as big as the little boy.

"Betty says we'll be there on Friday," Dad said in a firmer voice, seeming to gain strength when he spoke about coming to California to be with his family.

Dan and his wife, Susan, returned to the sheriff's office later that afternoon at the detective's request. They wanted one of us there when Dana arrived from Santa Clara. Dana first visited with the chaplain, and then the detectives told him in some detail what they knew at that point about the murders of his parents and sister at the family home on Easter Sunday.

Dana walked in wearing a baby-blue polo shirt, khakis, fashionable shoes, and a Rolex watch. He appeared tense, and his face was gaunt but absent of traces of tears or emotion. The detectives gave Dana details about what they had found at the family home earlier that day. He jerked back as if to get away when he was told his dad had been shot in the head from behind but didn't show the same reaction when hearing about his mother or sister.

"When did you last speak to your family?" Detective Souza asked Dana.

He replied, "Easter Sunday, when I left to return to school."

Souza followed with, "Did you try to contact them?"

"Yeah, several times," Dana replied, "but no one answered. I don't know anything about what happened," he added. I'm a victim too, you know. I've lost my whole family."

Dan was told by sheriff personnel that Dana had flown to Fresno on a private plane chartered by John Zent, an FBI agent who'd traveled with him. We had no idea who Zent was or his connection to Dana or the FBI. The deputies told Dan that Zent was the father of Monica Zent, Dana's classmate and friend at Santa Clara University. We had never heard of her either. Upon arriving, Dana told the sheriff detectives he had last seen his parents and sister on Easter Sunday, April 19, as he said goodbye to them at the Pajaro Dunes beach house.

Dana said he had spent the Saturday evening before Easter with Monica, her parents, and his mom, dad, and sister at the beach house. He said this was the first time his parents had met Monica or her parents. He went on to explain that Monica and her parents left late that Saturday night to drive back to their home in Morgan Hill while he stayed at Pajaro Dunes. On the morning of Easter Sunday, he said he played tennis with his dad, went for a walk on the beach with his mom, dad, and sister, and then ate brunch together. He said he left Sunday afternoon to return to his dorm at Santa Clara University.

On Wednesday night, April 22, the representative from the Whitehurst Funeral Home arrived at Dan's house. Richard and I were there, but not Dana. The representative gave us several possible choices for the funeral and asked if we knew whether Dale and Glee had wills with burial instructions.

It had only been one day since we'd learned about the murders, and already we were planning the details of the funeral. I was still in shock, as were my brothers. I said I would try to locate the wills. The funeral home representative told us to go to the Belmont Cemetery the next day to check out available burial plots and to try to find the wills. We would talk again soon. The cemetery was located on the wrong side of the tracks in the most run-down part of Fresno.

We asked Dana to come with us to the cemetery the next day. Dan, Richard, and I took Dan's car, and Dana drove separately. Upon arriving, the four of us crowded into a small office where the cemetery manager introduced herself and asked about our wishes regarding burial plots. She suggested a location near some large pine trees. I really felt like the youngest brother at that time. Dan, and Richard to a lesser extent, did most of the talking. Dan, now the eldest brother, spoke in a voice that seemed clear and in control, while mine was tentative and weak.

"Keep in mind there can be no headstones," the cemetery manager said in a businesslike manner. "We don't allow them." I was trying to adjust my thoughts to the flat markers, unlike the individually designed monuments at the Brighton, Ohio, cemetery where Mom and other relatives lay buried.

"That way it's easy for mowing over," she continued.

While I was thinking this showed a lack of respect, she was focused only on the cost savings and the speed with which the grass could be mowed. When the manager asked if we wanted a traditional in-ground burial, Dana spoke up and suggested cremation for all three.

Dan interrupted. "I don't think Dale would want to be cremated."

Dana offered to negotiate. "How about cremating Glee and Tiffany and do what you want with Dale?"

He never used the words "Mom," "Dad," or "my sister," just their first names. His voice was cold and detached. In the end, Dana got his wish. Glee and Tiffany were cremated, and in Dana's words, "We did what we wanted with our oldest brother." Dale's body remained in a coffin with an in-ground burial.

Then we talked about flowers. "Since there's only going to be one plot, do you want a flower container?" the office manager inquired.

"How much is it?" Dana asked.

"Thirty-five dollars," she replied.

"Why bother? I'm not going to see it anyway," Dana said.

I couldn't believe what he just said. He'd spoken abruptly without emotion, as if it were a business transaction. It seemed strange for him to be so aloof after his three family members had been murdered.

My brother Dan interjected, "Yeah, we want the container."

Back at Dan's house, I called my office and checked for messages. Mike Dowling, a Fresno attorney and law school classmate, had returned my call about Dale and Glee's will. When I called him back, he said he felt very bad about what happened to our family.

"Ben, I do have their wills. Glee called me a few years ago, saying you recommended that she see me about estate planning. I drew up the wills, but there are no burial instructions." Dowling said he would leave a copy of the wills for me with his office receptionist.

Knowing Betty and Dad would arrive from Cleveland Friday afternoon, we set the funeral for Saturday morning. The funeral home staff wanted to know the location and who would be involved in the service. Growing up, we had always attended the little white clapboard Congregational church in Brighton, Ohio, and we knew Dale and Glee had some kind of a relationship with the First Congregational Church (or Big Red Church, as it was known) in Fresno. We decided to split the funeral service, with an early unannounced Saturday morning service at the cemetery for family to avoid reporters, and later the same day, a public service at the First Congregational Church.

Dowling mentioned I should call Marv Baxter, a Hastings Law School classmate of ours, who was from Fresno but now living in San Francisco, serving as a justice of the California Supreme Court. Marv and his wife, Jane, had been longtime friends of Dale and Glee, and had occasionally babysat Dana and Tiffany when they were young.

After briefly discussing what had happened, I asked Marv if he would be willing to speak at the funeral. "Yes," he said, "I'll help in any way I can."

Dan and I also talked about having someone help us with

security at the funeral on Saturday, as a precautionary measure. I called Luke Temple, a private investigator introduced to me years ago by Ed Hunt when I was receiving threats during my divorce. At six-five and well over two hundred pounds, he had a commanding presence. I said, "We don't know what's going on here. Maybe we're all a target. Three family members have already been killed. Could you ride with us to the funeral?"

"Sure, I'll help out," he agreed.

I asked his fee.

"I'm not going to charge you," Luke said. He didn't ask for anything, but Dan slipped a hundred-dollar bill into Luke's suit coat pocket after the funeral service.

Hundreds of millions have died before and will in the future, but when the event involves someone close to you, that one occasion is singled out in your mind as if it had never happened before. We could not grieve these deaths alone, quietly and away from others, as there was so little time and space to reflect. There was constant publicity on the local radio and television and in the newspaper. I kept everything turned off at home so my sons wouldn't see or hear the news. I wanted to explain to the boys what I knew without them hearing it first on TV. National magazines were trying to contact the family to obtain interviews. Reporters showed up at Dan's driveway gate, but he didn't let them through. Dan found a business card stuck to his front gate from a *Fresno Bee* reporter and a handwritten note from Mark Arax, a reporter for the *Los Angeles Times,* asking Dan to call him, which Dan didn't do. Death, when stripped of emotion as it was with this situation, is cold, businesslike, and matter-of-fact, at least to others, and that was what we faced.

Luke met us at Dan's house Saturday morning after the private service, and except for Big Glee, we all rode in funeral home cars to the church service. Glee's mother and her caretaker left to return to her rest home residence in Lodi. Having Luke with us turned out to be a good thing, as television camera trucks and reporters were already lined up on Van Ness Boulevard near the front entrance of the First Congregational Church. Luke told our driver to go behind the church so the family could enter out of view of the media. Even then, a couple of cameramen ran around to the back of the church. When he saw them, Luke got out of the car, pulled up his big frame to what seemed like seven feet tall, and put up his arms.

"Get back!" he yelled. "Give these folks some privacy."

We waited together in a small parlor at the First Congregational Church. When summoned, we entered the church sanctuary in single file as a family with Suzy, my fiancée, and my two boys; Dan, his wife, Susan, and his two boys; Dad, Betty, Richard, and Dana. I glanced back at the sanctuary, which was completely filled, and saw many others standing, both inside and out. We took our seats in the front two rows of the hard wooden pews, just like the ones at the little church in Ohio before Dale paid to replace them with new cushioned ones. Cynically, I wondered whether the huge attendance resulted from morbid curiosity or respect for our family, or maybe some of both. Mom's role of organist at our little Congregational church in Ohio came to mind as I glanced up at the huge pipe organ being played softly.

Speaking at the service, Justice Baxter recalled his family's long friendship with Dale and Glee. He spoke of Glee's hard work and devotion to several community causes. As the service continued, Betty read individual notes that Dan, Richard, and I had written about one of our family members. I wanted to stand up and read my own note about Glee but told Betty I didn't think I could do it without breaking down. I had written about her love for books, politics, and travel. I mentioned that both she and Dale, while successful, were down-to-earth people who worked on their ranches together, driving the tractor and building fences.

Just before Pastor Frank Baldwin spoke, the sanctuary filled with the Roberta Flack song "The First Time Ever I Saw Your Face." Although a popular song, it seemed almost spiritual that day and brought back to me memories of Dale and Glee and our times together. Grief washed over me like a wave. Hearing some clearing of throats and sniffles as the song continued, I turned around in my seat and recognized some folks looking down to avoid eye contact with me. Baxter mentioned in his remarks that Glee had told him and his wife years earlier about the song's meaning to her and Dale. It reminded them of their meeting at a dance in Arizona, when Glee, a student at the Thunderbird School of Foreign Trade near Phoenix, met Dale, an Air Force jet pilot stationed nearby. That day, the song and its words reflected their first meeting.

After the service, our family and funeral guests gathered for a reception in the church's Fellowship Hall. We didn't know at the time that plainclothes sheriff detectives were attending the funeral looking for anything that might provide clues. We noticed something odd about Dana that day. As he shook hands in the receiving line along with other family members, thanking those who attended the service, he commented on the size of a woman's diamond ring as guests moved through the line.

"What a rock," he said to the guest. Hearing Dana's remark, I stepped back from the reception line and looked away, needing to distance myself from Dana's inappropriate behavior.

When we arrived back at Dan's house, we made plans for Dad and Betty's return to Ohio. Dad told me he wanted to do one thing before leaving for home in Ohio. "I want to talk to the sheriff."

I set up a meeting with Sheriff Steve Magarian, whom I knew through politics. He was a big, friendly guy and agreed to see Dad. When we met, he seemed, as Dad said to me later, "as honest as the day is long." He quietly reassured Dad that with him, this whole mess—the loss of human life and the mystery of what happened to our family—was in very good hands. As we left his office, Dad looked up at the sheriff, who towered over him.

"You need to solve this," Dad said.

"I will, I will," the sheriff replied, and we left.

The next day, Betty flew home to Ohio. Dad, completely heartbroken, decided to stay in Fresno for a few days. His usual smile and good humor were gone. He seemed lost in his own thoughts and stopped talking to us.

I asked Dad, "Can we get a prescription for you that might help?"

He replied, "I don't think it would do any good." Then he added, "Dale has never done anything wrong. I know him. Why would somebody do this to him?"

"Dad," I said, "there's no answer."

As Dad grew more despondent, Dan called our doctor and asked for something to help Dad's emotional decline. After we picked up the prescription for Dad, he agreed to start taking the pills, and they seemed to help.

Dad had always been strong and never afraid, but this experience was his undoing. Betty couldn't wait to leave Fresno and flew home to Ohio the next day. She returned only once, six years later.

► THE INVESTIGATION

Several weeks after the funeral, Glee's two eighty-something-year-old aunts, Helen and Grace, along with their two dogs, arrived in Fresno from Oklahoma in a huge motor home. The two had driven cross-country to Fresno by themselves. They parked the motor home in Dan's driveway and hooked up the power through his garage. These two women, sisters to Glee's mother,

Big Glee, had plenty of stories to tell of their Oklahoma life and their company, which oversaw the gas and oil lease business inherited from their father. Dan knew them from a trip he had made to Oklahoma with Dale, but Richard and I had never met them.

The two aunts wasted no time before asking about the details of what had happened. Dan suggested we invite Detective John Phillip Souza of the Fresno Sheriff's Office to meet with us. While Chris Curtis, Ernie Burke, and many others from the sheriff's department worked on the case, Souza was in charge and set the tone of the murder investigation for case FSC 92-15285.

Souza looked and acted like the dark-complected Columbo television character. Outwardly somewhat unpolished and tough, he was nevertheless savvy and full of street smarts. This rather short, stocky detective came across as friendly with his mustache and a rumpled look. As soon as he arrived at Dan's house, he asked for and was given a beer.

Drinking beer and talking at the same time, Helen, Grace, Dan, Richard, and I sat in the motor home and listened late into the night as Detective Souza described what the officers had learned so far.

Souza said they'd pieced together that fifty-nine-year-old Dale, flying alone from the Watsonville airport near the Pajaro Dunes beach house, had landed his twin-engine Beechcraft at the Fresno air terminal at 3:22 in the afternoon on Easter Sunday, according to the air traffic control tower log. He had made the short flight from takeoff to landing in about an hour. Dale went first to his company office at Western Piper Sales, located next to one of the runways at the Fresno International Airport. There he called his secretary, Marlene Reid, at her home to ask for help in finding an office file. Marlene later told the detectives that the file involved an ongoing dispute with the owner of an airplane being serviced by Dale's company. According to Marlene, Dale had impounded the plane because of unpaid repair bills, and the plane's owner, who claimed the work hadn't been done right, was livid about the matter.

According to Souza, they determined that Glee and Tiffany had left the Pajaro Dunes beach house for home in Glee's Cadillac, a two-and-a-half-hour drive, some time before Dale's departure. A short distance from their Fresno home, Glee stopped at a Fosters Freeze store, and Tiffany bought an ice cream float.

Souza went on, "Based on what we found, Glee and her daughter arrived at their home before Dale. We found Glee's Cadillac parked in the garage with the trunk open, luggage still inside, and the garage door down. An older Jeep Wagoneer parked in the driveway of their home was unlocked and had a garage opener attached to the driver's side visor. Tiffany appeared to have entered the house before her mother using the door from the garage. Glee would later enter the house through the same door.

"Maria, Dale and Glee's housekeeper," Souza continued, "told us she regularly came to their house on Tuesday mornings and had a key to the front door and the code to the alarm system. When she arrived on Tuesday, April twenty-first, two days after Easter Sunday, Frank Knapp, Dale and Glee's next-door neighbor, met Maria at the front door before she could enter. Knapp had received a call from Dana saying he was at school in Santa Clara and had grown concerned about his parents when he hadn't heard from them since Easter Sunday. He told Knapp, 'No one answers the home phone.'"

Maria then opened the front door that Tuesday morning with her key and was surprised to find the alarm disarmed, something she had never encountered before. After opening the front door of the Spanish-style home, she could see the kitchen door was closed, also something unusual. Knapp then entered the house

21

while Maria waited outside. After seeing a body on the kitchen floor, he backed out of the house, told Maria not to go in, and went back to his house to call the sheriff's office.

Responding to Knapp's call that morning, the detectives found twenty-four-year-old Tiffany lying facedown in the dining area of the kitchen. She wore sneakers, a cotton shirt, and light blue Levi's. Her body lay in a pool of dried blood, her hand clutching a Fosters Freeze cup. She had taken one shot to the back of her head and had fallen forward facedown with her arms pinned under her.

The detectives found fifty-seven-year-old Glee lying on her side, faceup, next to some file cabinets in the home's office off the main hallway about halfway between the garage entry door and Tiffany's body. She was wearing tennis shoes, jeans, a sweatshirt with the words "Pajaro Dunes" on the front, and a Patek Philippe watch on her left wrist that the coroner later removed. She had been shot more than once in the face and body at close range by someone standing over her with a gun. Glee's arms were stretched across her face in an apparent attempt to shield herself from the shooter. She was lying on the dried, blood-soaked carpet.

They found our brother Dale's body lying facedown in the hallway just inside the door leading from the garage. He was still clutching some mail and newspapers, while others were scattered in front of him along with his broken sunglasses. He had been shot once in the back of the head and neck area and, like Tiffany, had fallen facedown with his arms pinned under his chest. His Levi's and polo shirt were soaked in dried blood.

The house had been ransacked, with dresser drawers open and clothes strewn around the bedroom. Piles of electronics equipment and VCR tapes were stacked up on the bedsheets. Souza mentioned that at most robbery scenes, items to be stolen are stuffed in pillowcases, not laid out on sheets.

On Dale and Glee's master bedroom wall hung large pictures

of Dana and Tiffany. On the bed, detectives found an open box of nine-millimeter bullets with some missing.

After the group consumed more beer, Souza finished describing the crime scene and left Dan's place. This detailed crime description seemed detached from me, as if he were not talking about our family members. The tragedy was still an abstract event, yet the descriptions of the victims caused me to picture them in my mind, both before and after being shot. *Did they feel or see anything before their last breath?* I wondered.

Tuesday afternoon, after arriving in Fresno with John Zent and meeting at the sheriff's office, Dana rode to Dan and Susan's home, where Dan suggested that Dana stay with them and help out with the funeral arrangements. Dana did stay with them until the funeral. In the driveway of Dan's house, I asked Dana if I could help him. "No," he replied, "I have everything right here." He was carrying a plastic see-through bag with several colorful polo shirts, some with the store tags still attached, and a leather toiletry bag. Dana said he could sleep in one of the basement bedrooms of Dan's house; as soon as he got to the basement room, he closed the door.

Monica and her mother arrived in Fresno later that day from their home in Morgan Hill, driving a Mercedes. Monica stayed at Dan's house with Dana in a basement bedroom and left in the evening to be with her parents. Mr. and Mrs. Zent stayed in the condo belonging to the parents of my fiancée, Suzy Harris, who were out of town at the time. When Suzy and I stopped by to see the Zents that night, John Zent was sprawled on the couch, wearing a colorful Hawaiian-print shirt and watching what appeared to be a murder episode of a crime show on television. "Did you ever see this show?" he asked me.

"No, I don't think I have," I replied.

"Well, you should sometime. It's well done."

He didn't talk about the murders that had brought him to

Fresno. He was confident and didn't appear distressed or out-wardly concerned—certainly not like a man whose daughter's boyfriend had just learned his family had all been killed.

On Wednesday, the following day, I called Dan and told him I had the will but no burial instructions. "Dana's been asking about the wills," Dan said. "I'll tell him you have them and can come by tonight for dinner, and we'll all go over them."

The three Zents, Dana, Richard, and I were sitting at Dan's large, circular, glass-topped table with a deer antler chandelier hanging overhead. After we finished eating dinner, Dan suggested we go to the master bedroom to look over the wills. Dan, Richard, Dana, and I started for the bedroom, and John Zent followed.

Dana told Zent that he should stay outside, which he did.

With everyone assembled, I started to speak up and said both wills provided that in the event of Dale and Glee's death, everything they had would go equally to Dana and Tiffany. With Tiffany now gone, everything would go to Dana. I explained that under the terms of the will, the estate would pass into a trust, and Dana, who was twenty-one at the time, would not get the balance of the trust until he was thirty-five. Hearing this, Dana lurched forward in his chair.

"Why would my dad do this to me?" he blurted out, using the term "dad" for the first time during the ordeal.

"I'm sure he wanted you to wait until you were old enough to manage the money," I replied.

The quick exchange and Dana's angry outburst that night ended the meeting, and we left Dan's bedroom.

On June 18, 1992, the Fresno County Sheriff's Office issued an unusual press release, announcing a $25,000 reward for the kill-ers of the Dale Ewell family. It included an additional detail that "none of the victims were molested." Apparently, someone had started a rumor the sheriff felt needed to be addressed.

Dan, Richard, and I agreed to contribute more money to the reward fund and announced it would be doubled to $50,000. Dan asked Dana about participating with us in the reward increase, but he begged off, saying something to the effect he thought it would be a waste of time and money.

The investigation continued, and a couple of months later, Dan, Richard, and I were each interviewed separately at the sheriff's office by one of the detectives. The primary questioning involved what we had each been doing on that Easter Sunday afternoon of the murders. They also wanted to know if we had any information that might help them solve the case.

I told the detective that I'd been home on Easter Sunday planting flowers that I'd purchased earlier that day at Orchard Supply Hardware. I didn't know of anything else that would be helpful.

The investigations continued. On June 11, 1995, three years after the murders, the sheriff's office issued an unusual and terse statement, prompted at the request of Mike Dowling, Dale and Glee's estate lawyer.

The statement read: "After lengthy investigations and deliberations with the Fresno County District Attorney's office, it is the position of our department that Dana Ewell is to be considered a prime suspect in the investigation." I didn't know about it beforehand. This brought down the curtain on rumors of drug dealing, foreign hit men, and CIA operatives being involved in the murders. Detectives continued their around-the-clock surveillance of Dana, the family house, and the activity there. The detectives told us he was spending money from a life insurance policy that had been released to him outside of the trust, and, while under surveillance, he had been seen going into a bank with another male, both of whom were smiling and high-fiving each other. Dana also went to Dale's airplane dealership and told employees he was in charge.

Mike Dowling, who had taken on the role of executor and attorney for the estate, spoke with me about Dana's actions and his desire to get money released prematurely. Dowling started to meet frequently with my brothers and me about the estate and told us that Dana would come to his law office late at night, sometimes with another young man, and let himself in using an office key Dowling had loaned him. The office records showed Dana made numerous phone calls to places all over the United States and to foreign locations including Switzerland.

Dad, always good at sizing up a situation, told me he'd called Dale and Glee's residence phone number to see if Dana would answer, checking on the rumor from Richard that Dana had moved back in and was living at home. Dad left messages on the answering machine for Dana to call him. A few minutes later, Dana would call back, saying Dad's call had been forwarded to him at his dorm room at Santa Clara University. Dad knew he had caught Dana lying because Richard had gone out to Dale's house at the time of Dad's calls and found Dana living there. There were still bullet holes in the walls, and the bloodstained carpets had been torn up and removed but not yet replaced.

Dad said to me, "Ben, there something not right about Dana and what happened. I know he's lying to me."

"Did you say anything to him?" I asked.

"I didn't want to confront him," Dad replied. "What good would that do?"

Dad expressed his belief that Dana may have been involved in the crime. After discussing it with me, I arranged for him to meet with Ron Freeman, a local Ohio attorney whom I first met while working on a road crew. Ron changed Dad's will to state, "I deliberately make no provision for Dana Ewell," and made me executor. The eventual outcome of Dale's death would be that, if Dana could not inherit under California law because of his involvement in the crime, Dale's estate would go to Dad.

Dana flew back to Ohio to visit Dad, a strategy the detectives thought was an attempt to garner favor with the family. Unfortunately, Dad had told his grandson not to make the long flight from California as he was not welcome and would not be allowed in the house. Dana flew to Ohio anyway, but when he arrived at Dad's house in his rental car, Dad met him in the driveway, and he got no farther. A couple of summers earlier, Dale and Dana had flown to Ohio to visit Dad, something Dale did every year. Dale thought Dana could spend the summer with his grandfather, but it didn't work out well or for very long. Dana left for home, complaining about having to sleep downstairs in the basement, even though Dale had fixed it up for Dana to have his own space.

Dad died in 1994, and before his death, he changed his will to name Betty as executor. After Dad's death, Dowling informed us that Dana wanted money released from his parents' estate. My brothers and I wanted to prevent that since the sheriff's department now suspected Dana of being involved in the crime. Dan arranged for Russ Georgenson, a Fresno attorney, to represent the three of us and attempt to block Dana from getting any money while he was being investigated as a suspect. Betty told Dowling that she was willing to release money to Dana from Dale's estate as he and his lawyers had requested. Dan, Richard, and I hired Russ Georgenson to go to court to prevent Betty from releasing any funds to Dana, as Dale's money had to now pass through Dad's estate. Fresno Superior Court Judge Henery held a hearing and denied our request to stop the distribution to Dana. We then hired an Ohio attorney to represent us. The lawyers for Dana mentioned in court that Dana needed the money "for his defense, not to go to Hawaii." Our plan to stop the distribution of money was all over the newspapers. Thinking selfishly, I said to Dan, "I'm not sure what would be worse, not finding the killer or finding out the killer is part of our own family."

With a big brother's admonition, Dan replied, "Don't be ridiculous, Ben; we have to find out either way, no matter what grief and bad publicity we will go through."

The judge in Ohio, using what we thought was better Midwestern common sense than the one in Fresno, ruled that Betty, as executor of Dad's will, had to carry out Dad's wishes, and Dad had expressed those wishes by deliberately excluding Dana from any bequest. This, according to the Ohio judge, would preclude Betty from allowing distribution of funds to Dana. Although Betty felt Dana needed money for his defense, Dan, who had been suspicious about Dana from the first reports of the crime, felt just the opposite: that he shouldn't receive any money from the victims.

"Ben," Dan said to me, "something isn't right here. This kid is acting like nothing happened."

About this time, one of the detectives had noticed a *Fresno Bee* ad advertising fur coats for sale. They determined Dana had placed the ad trying to sell some of his deceased mother's clothing. The detectives told us that Dana had been driving his mother's Cadillac when it still had fingerprint dusting powder on it.

The investigation of case 92-15285 ground on for three years. The sheriff's personnel and others assigned to the case in addition to John Souza included Ernie Burke, Chris Curtice, Allen Boudreau, Jose Flores, Mindy Ybarra, Chris Caudle, and many others from that department including Margaret Mims, who was later elected sheriff. They worked tirelessly to solve the case.

On March 3, 1995, I got a call from a friend, George Baker, then executive editor of the local *Fresno Bee* newspaper. "Ben," he said, "they are at your brother Dale's house now with arrest warrants." Since shortly after the murders, Dana and his Santa Clara classmate, Joel Radovcich, had been living at Dale and Glee's house, but neither was there that evening.

A forty-six-page sworn declaration from the sheriff's office supported the four arrest warrants that were signed by my former law partner, Superior Court Judge Larry O'Neill. He mentioned to me later that he had been eating dinner with friends at his home that evening when the detectives arrived. He reviewed the declaration and signed the warrants for arrest of Joel Patrick Radovcich; Ernest Jack Ponce, a friend of Joel's from Los Angeles; Peter Radovcich, Joel's brother; and Dana James Ewell. All were eventually taken into custody.

▶ THE MURDER TRIAL

After three more years of legal maneuvering, news articles, and family turmoil, and six years from the date of the murders, the case of the People of the State of California vs. Dana James Ewell and Joel Patrick Radovcich came to trial in Fresno Superior Court before the Honorable Frank Creede, an acquaintance of mine from our days attending Republican political events.

Although a lawyer with some limited trial experience, I was not prepared for what took place in the courtroom at the murder trial. Dan, Richard, and I were all called by the prosecution to testify on behalf of the State of California at the trial and again during the penalty phase of the case. My sister flew out to California and testified too, but it was for the defense of Dana Ewell. Why Betty wanted to help in Dana's defense we never fully understood. I thought about the advice from District Attorney Ed Hunt: "Ben, if you need to find Jesus, look in a jail, as everyone there says they've found him." Was it her strong belief in God that convinced her that, during his three years in jail, Dana might have found faith? Was it a deep-seated dislike for her brothers who, when growing up, seemed always to be in the spotlight while she was in the background being raised to Mom's strict and sometimes unreasonable standards? She never said her reasons. When I tried to speak to her about it in later years, she just repeated Mom's frequent expression, "This too shall pass."

My testimony centered around the reading of the will in my brother Dan's bedroom in 1992, three days after the murders. Dana's defense attorney took the position that it wouldn't make sense for him to kill his parents since he wasn't going to get the money for fourteen more years. To attack the defense's theory, my testimony on the witness stand for the prosecution was evidence to prove that when the will was first read and explained to Dana, his response indicated he hadn't known he'd have to wait fourteen years to get the money.

Even though I knew Judge Creede quite well, he showed me no courtesy or mercy on the witness stand. When I was answering, I purposely kept talking after he admonished me by slamming down a law book onto his bench and saying, "We have jail cells across the street for people like you who are in contempt of court."

Betty was called to the witness stand by Dana's lawyer to impeach the testimony of her brothers. She testified that none of her brothers could be completely trusted or believed, especially Dan. I thought this was odd for her to say, yet I didn't dwell upon it. Dan, however, was devastated and never spoke to Betty again. I did speak with and visit Betty several times over the years, but we never discussed the crime, her testimony, or Dana.

The detectives explained that, like most criminals, Dana had wanted to validate himself by having others believe in him. The detectives said Dana tried to get Betty to believe he had nothing to do with the crime and that perhaps, since her brothers might benefit, they may have been involved. Prior to any of this, Betty had always helped anyone she thought was in need or had a problem. This time it was Dana, and she seemed intent on helping him. She arrived in Fresno from Ohio with her daughter-in-law in time to testify at the trial. Did she truly believe he had nothing to do with the crime? I would never know. The trial continued with Dan, his wife, Susan, and Richard attending often, while I stayed away. Judge Creede told me years later, "Sorry I had to be so rough on you, but because of our acquaintance, I couldn't show any bias toward you."

As the evidence in the murder trial unfolded, the prosecution presented the case that Dana Ewell had engaged Joel Radovcich to shoot Dana's parents and sister so they could split the eight-million-dollar estate. Jack Ponce, although personally involved, testified as a witness for the prosecution and was given immunity. A student at UCLA, Ponce said he wanted to buy a van, needed money, and purchased the van and an AT-9 assault rifle used in the crime with money Joel gave him. Detectives learned later the money actually came from Dana. Ponce testified in detail about the crime as told to him by Joel Radovcich, sometimes with vulgar language. Ponce repeated what Joel told him about his role in the killing, saying, "If there's a God, I'm fucked." Joel Radovcich drilled holes in the barrel of the assault rifle in his family's garage in Los Angeles and covered the holes with tennis balls to create a homemade silencer. He entered Dale and Glee's home after dark the night before Easter Sunday, letting himself in with a key located where Dana had said it was hidden and disarming the alarm with the code Dana had given him. He stayed overnight in the vacant house and waited on a sheet of plastic he'd brought with him to avoid leaving clues.

He had completely shaved all his body hair, wore rubber gloves, and waited until the family came home Easter Sunday afternoon. Joel told Ponce that after shooting each of them as they entered the house, he could hear a gurgle in their throats as they

31

lay dying. He remained in the house with the bodies until it was dark. He then left the house, went to his parked car, and returned to the Los Angeles area.

According to Ponce, Peter Radovcich, Joel's brother, helped get rid of the evidence of the crime by driving around the hills of Los Angeles and throwing the plastic sheet, gloves, shells, and tennis balls out the car window. One piece of evidence wasn't thrown out but was kept by Jack Ponce. It was the only piece of evidence from the crime scene ever found by the detectives. The gun barrel of the assault rifle used in the crime had been buried by Ponce in a vacant lot near Peter Radovcich's Los Angeles apartment.

After his arrest and hearing from the detectives that he faced the death penalty, Ponce agreed to cooperate with the detectives and spoke to them about the crime. Ponce led the detectives to the vacant lot in Los Angeles, where they dug up the rusty gun barrel he had buried there almost six years before. Ballistic tests showed the barrel markings of the AT-9 assault rifle fitted with the homemade silencer matched the bullets found embedded in the victims' bodies and the floors and walls of Dale and Glee's home.

On May 12, 1998, six months after the trial started and almost exactly six years after the murders, the jury reached unanimous verdicts of guilty of murder in the first degree with special circumstances for Dana James Ewell and Joel Patrick Radovcich for the murders of Dale Alan Ewell, Glee Ethel Ewell, and Tiffany Ann Ewell. Ponce was granted immunity on his murder charges in exchange for his testimony on behalf of the prosecution, and the court dismissed Peter Radovcich's charges at the prosecution's request.

After the trial itself, each of my brothers and I, along with Dan's wife, Susan, testified in the penalty phase of the case where victims' families are permitted to describe their personal relationship with the victims and the impact on them resulting from the victims' death. Susan spoke on behalf of Tiffany, Dan and Richard on behalf of Dale, and I spoke on behalf of Glee. Dan testified in somber tones how Dale was really his big brother in so many ways. Both older and bigger than Dan, Dale also mentored Dan in business. Richard told how Dale had helped him financially when he was in tough times after his divorce. I spoke about Glee's love for travel, books, and politics. I mentioned her activities and service to the community.

About a month later, the same jury during the penalty phase of the case voted 11-1 for the death penalty for Dana and 10-2 for the death penalty for Joel, resulting in a hung jury on the penalty phase, as there was no unanimous verdict. Ed Hunt, still Fresno County District Attorney, met with Dan, Richard, and me about the hung jury and expressed his willingness to retry the penalty phase of the case to seek what he described as the probable outcome of a death penalty verdict. He said, however, it would be up to the three of us if we wanted to go ahead with another penalty phase trial. After a lot of discussion, we decided not to ask the next jury to put Dana and Joel to death and said to Hunt and television reporters, "It has gone on long enough."

Dana and Joel received a sentence of three consecutive life terms in prison without the possibility of parole. I really didn't want to go through the penalty trial again and have to hear and relive all the gruesome details. By this time, Betty had gone back to Ohio and never returned to California.

After over one million dollars was deducted for Dowling's attorney's fees and payment of estate taxes, the Salvation Army, as directed by Glee's will, received one-half of the remaining estate including the airplane business, the ranches, eighteen separate savings accounts containing $100,000 each, and other assets. Glee had told Dowling years before at the time her will was written that when her dad was living in Chicago as a young man, he had been helped by the Salvation Army. The other half went to Dale's four siblings. We were told later that Betty refused her share and gave her distribution to the lawyer who defended Dana. This made Betty's actions seem even stranger, especially to my brothers. I thought Betty's decision to disclaim her inheritance might have been her way to express that she wanted nothing to do with the case or any money associated with the tragedy.

I found that while Dale and Glee had been very well known and well liked, they were also very private. Many said later they were "very best friends and knew them well," something I doubted. On the other hand, many said they "knew for sure" that Dana would turn out to be trouble, something I also doubted. After an incident we tend to adjust facts to fit the situation.

I tried to make some sense of the tragedy, or "waste of life," as Dad had first described it. Our Ohio cousin, ninety-year-old Bruce Murray, a former college professor with a PhD in chemistry, said to me in his plain Midwest language, "Killing your parents is a stupid thing to do."

I went to see Ed Hunt after the trial in search of some lesson or meaning and hopefully to shed some light on the matter. After all, Ed had been connected to my family from the beginning of the murder through the long investigation and trial. I suspected that because he himself was a pilot, he may have felt a kinship to Dale.

Being a very smart, savvy Alabama boy, Ed would eventually serve five consecutive terms as district attorney fueled by his own statement to me: "I'll keep getting reelected unless they catch me screwing a small animal in Courthouse Park." Ed, always a colorful talker with profanity that was more amusing than offensive, gave his condensed version of motivation for the senseless tragedy, "Ben, the problem today is people would rather chase after money than pussy."

I didn't respond. I just thought about the other times in my life when I wanted to hear words of wisdom from a knowledgeable person and was disappointed. But maybe, in his own crude way, Ed had gotten to the crux of the matter.

Chapter 2

SUNDAY AFTERNOON
ON THE FARM

I'm ten years old, slouched in a hammock stretched between two Bartlett pear trees along the west side of our house on a Sunday afternoon. A breeze out of the west from the direction of Charlie Leider's place was rocking my hammock back and forth. Years later when my Sundays included living among the Haight-Ashbury hippies in the 1960s, the murder of my brother and his family, and Dad's final breath in the Cleveland Metro Burn Unit, I often thought about those peaceful times on the farm.

Our two-story, white clapboard house sat back about two hundred feet from Zenobia Road, a dirt and gravel, single-travel lane that ran east and west in Huron County, Ohio. The westerly end of the road came to a dead end at Clarksfield Hollow, a crossroads with a store, tavern, and Seventh-day Adventist church at the intersection of Ohio State Highway 18 and Zenobia. The easterly end of the road was at our farm, which served as the boundary between Huron County where we lived and neighboring Lorain County. Huron County, a rural, poor, sparsely inhabited area, contrasted sharply with the more urban, wealthier, and populated Lorain County.

From the Philco radio next to the open window in our front room, I could hear from my hammock the muffled voice of the play-by-play announcer and the occasional roar of the crowd from a Cleveland Indians baseball game. The Indians won the 1948 World Series, and boys I knew at school could later name the team's entire starting player lineup for that year. We would continue to hope for the next championship, which, over seventy years later, still hasn't happened.

Mom's black upright Baldwin piano leaned against one wall of our front room. I often awoke to her playing it and singing. She especially liked hymns and often sang along while playing one of her favorites, "In the Garden." I could hear her singing the words, "I come to the garden alone, while the dew is still on the roses," from my bedroom. The sound of the piano, Mom's voice, and those words are still in my mind today when I close my eyes and think of those times. Years later, Dad bought Mom a small electric organ that we gathered around as a family and sang while Mom played other favorites like "Onward, Christian Soldiers."

Across from the piano were our Philco radio and Victrola record player. In the evenings when the daily farmwork, housework, and caring for five kids came to an end, Mom carefully took out her black vinyl 78 rpm Enrico Caruso records kept in the mahogany-colored, four-legged music stand and listened to the Italian tenor on the Victrola late into the night.

The Philco radio fascinated me. It could receive shortwave radio signals from around the world by finely tuning three separate black rotating dials. Each dial could be turned individually or all together by engaging a metal bracket. Dad had strung a copper antenna wire from the radio, through an opening at the bottom of a front room window, up to the tin roof, and across to a brick chimney. Although I couldn't understand the foreign voices coming from the large, felt-covered radio speaker, I thought about the

37

faraway places in Europe or Asia where they must have originated. Our cousin Ray only a few years before had returned from fighting Japan in the South Pacific during World War II. Our only knowledge of those places would come from newspaper headlines and newsreels that made them no less mysterious.

Betty, the oldest and only girl of us five kids, slept in the downstairs bedroom off the front room. Rather short, plainly dressed, and usually without makeup, since Mom discouraged her from wearing any, Betty made up for any physical shortcomings with her outgoing personality, intelligence, and high energy. Although she was twelve years older than I, I felt close to Betty because we both loved the outdoors and the trees, plants, and flowers we found there, and we shared a passion for reading and collecting books.

There were two other bedrooms downstairs off the dining room, Mom and Dad's small room and my even smaller room measuring only about eight by ten feet, just enough for a small single bed and a little four-drawer dresser. My only window looked out over our sandstone block front porch to the front yard and Zenobia Road. My three brothers slept upstairs, each in his own separate room. The biggest room belonged to the biggest and oldest brother, Dale, a six-foot, three-inch high school basketball and baseball star with the Brighton High School Rangers. Dale, the team captain, played center on the basketball team and outfield on the baseball team. He made a legendary catch over the outfield fence at a championship baseball game, which both won the game and broke his right arm. I was ten years younger than Dale and served as the team mascot in a western-style red shirt, red pants, two matching cap guns, a white fake leather holster, and matching cowboy boots. Dale's high school girlfriend, Alice, served as head cheerleader for the Rangers and helped me with my costume and to get over my fear of going out on the gym floor with the cheerleaders at halftime.

Dale covered his bedroom walls with posters of World War II fighter planes and hung several of his hand-carved balsa wood model airplanes from the ceiling. He was flying or thinking about flying most of his life. An old black-and-white photo I found shows Mom and all five kids hanging on our 1939 Ford with Dale on the running board holding a model airplane he had built. He joined a flying club in college and flew the club's single-engine Stinson airplane home to the farm, landing on the soybean field on the west side of our house. To get the neighbors' attention, Dan, Richard and I, with Dale's consent, wheeled the plane from the soybean field down Zenobia Road and parked it in our front yard. Dale used to say that any landing you walk away from is a good one, and after he crashed the club airplane and knocked out his front teeth, his flying continued in the Air Force with jets and later executive luxury planes. Flying was Dale's passion and would be until his very last flight. He was inquisitive, always wanting to explore and learn new things, a trait I admired and wanted to emulate. He spread out maps of the solar system on our kitchen table to study the location of the planets. He converted the small closet at the top of the stairs into a darkroom to develop the photographs he was always taking while the smell of developing fluid lingered upstairs. I tried to be like Dale. He always worked hard, helped Dad and Mom, and didn't complain or get upset about things.

My other two brothers, twins Richard and Rolland, each had his own separate upstairs room. They didn't look or act anything alike. Richard was about six feet tall with dark hair and an outgoing personality that differed completely from Dan. Though Richard was called "Dick" at home, and in high school and college, Mom phoned me one night to tell me of a change.

"He wants to be called 'Richard' now."

"Why?" I asked.

"Just do it and don't ask why."

I didn't ask, as Mom cautioned. Mom didn't mince words, take time to answer questions about why things happened, or waste time gossiping with others. She spoke out about anyone she thought wrong on principle, including our high school principal, whom she described as "nothing but a pantywaist." I never knew for sure what the word meant, but it sounded derogatory when applied to a man.

Richard served as high school senior class president and valedictorian, as well as college homecoming king at Miami University in southern Ohio. He was outgoing and always friendly to others, including me. The difference in temperaments, personalities, and ambitions I saw early in my brothers continued throughout their lives.

Richard's twin, my brother Rolland, always known by the nickname "Dan," stood shorter than Richard. He was blond, smart, athletic, and couldn't care less about being diplomatic. He was funny or sarcastic, depending on whether you were on the receiving end of his remarks. During his teenage years, he wrecked seven or eight cars, escaping with only minor injuries, got in fights, and more than once caused the county sheriff to come to our door late at night. He usually escaped punishment because of his excellent academic record, athletic ability, and personality. As tackle on the high school football team, he competed at the Ohio state championship level. He dated the coach's daughter, of whom he jokingly said, "Probably doesn't hurt my football career."

Dan could be so understanding and helpful to Mom and Dad and his brothers, but within earshot of non-family, he could become sarcastic and even mean-spirited. I always thought his inner self was different from his outer self and that he was probably really shy. On weekends, he often took me with him to the stock car racetrack in nearby Amherst. He didn't take off with friends and leave me behind but took me around with him and introduced me to other drivers and race car owners. "This is my little brother, Ben," he would say. I stayed right by his side in the hot, noisy, dangerous track pit. He owned an ether-enhanced, gasoline-fueled stock car that he only occasionally raced himself; usually he hired someone else to take the wheel. The car had no glass in the windows, and the doors had been welded shut to keep the driver securely inside. Crawling through the opening of the driver's side window was the only access to the car's interior. Sometimes Dan hauled the race car home to the farm on a trailer, and we took turns driving it around the neighborhood and across the fields to the amazement of our neighbors and friends.

Life on our farm was always busy. Each of us had chores to do. Taking care of the horses, cows, and even the pigs ranked high up the ladder of desirable farmwork, and those jobs went to my older brothers, leaving me with the chickens and the sheep. I had the job of gathering eggs from our leghorn and Rhode Island red chickens. The hens vigorously protected their eggs by pecking my hands and drawing blood. After gathering up the eggs in a wire mesh pail, I took them to the basement and helped Mom "candle" them by passing the eggs in front of a single light bulb hanging from the basement ceiling that would detect streaks of blood or cracks. Defective eggs, sometimes with a very small but visible chicken embryo, were put in a bucket to feed to the pigs that, as Dad said, "would eat anything." To feed the chickens every day, I took a bushel basket of ears of corn from the dilapidated crib and ran them through the hand-cranked corn sheller. As I turned the crank, it would spin two sets of sharp steel teeth in opposite directions, stripping the kernels from the cob into a pail to be fed to the chickens.

In addition to taking care of the chickens, as the youngest, I looked after the sheep. My older brothers raised heifers, took the animals to the Lorain County Fair in nearby Wellington, and won ribbons, and I wanted to do the same. I hoped to raise a lamb for that purpose. Thinking the sheep we had were not of ribbon-winning caliber, Dad asked around about purebred lambs for sale. He heard of a man in western Huron County near Norwalk who raised purebred Corriedales as a hobby. Dad said the man owned a lumberyard, probably had a lot of money, and might consider selling one of his lambs. Dad took me with him and drove our Ford pickup to the fancy entrance gate with a ValeVue Farm sign and up a long driveway to a big house on the top of a hill. The man seemed friendly, talking with Dad about my interest in trying to win a ribbon in the sheep judging contest at the Lorain County Fair. In the end, the man gave me a lamb to raise and refused to take any money. His generosity stuck in my mind that day. Someone with money would help me and ask nothing in return, and I wondered why. I had not yet formed the idea that some people get satisfaction and personal reward just from helping others. In later years, older and more cynical, I had other thoughts about such people. Did this generosity lessen the guilt they might have had in making money in the first place? Clearly, the observation did not apply to every generous person. There are just as many reasons for the generosity of others as there are generous people.

We raised pigs for sale and did our own butchering in a lot between our house and the horse barn, home to our two work horses, Prince and Bill. At that time, the US Conservation Service, an agency in the Department of Agriculture, gave farmers money to dig ponds, claiming they would be a good source of water for firefighting purposes. This same federal agency also gave money to farmers to grow fewer crops in order to keep prices high, as well as for soil amendments that resulted in bigger crop yields. Dad could never understand a government that paid him money to reduce crop production by not planting and at the same time gave him money to increase crop production. I began to question similar illogical thinking of people in charge. Sometimes the illogical thinking and actions of others can benefit you. If you do benefit from such a situation without harming others, and if it isn't something you can or should correct on your own, asking for forgiveness for receiving the benefit is not necessary.

On Sunday mornings, Dad would chop off the head of a chicken selected for the family dinner. Stretching the chicken's neck over a tree stump in the backyard, he whacked off the head with one chop from a hatchet. The body of the chicken, missing its head, would break loose and run around the yard for several minutes, spraying blood in all directions. Dad had firsthand knowledge when he used the phrase, "He's acting like a chicken with its head cut off," to describe someone behaving strangely.

On Sunday afternoons, the backbreaking daily grind of farmwork came almost to an end. After the Sunday morning service at Brighton Congregational Church and a dinner of fried chicken, mashed potatoes, sweet corn, pie, and in summer, fresh lettuce leaves covered with sugar, calm settled over our house and farm. Dad usually fell asleep in the big green chair in the front room. "I was just resting my eyes," he would say upon waking. For Sunday supper we ate only popcorn, Uncle Bob's bottled grape juice, and Mom's homemade chocolate fudge. We grew the popping corn in the field behind the big red barn. When the small orange-colored ears ripened, we put the corn in burlap sacks and hung them to dry from the rafters in the horse barn. We shelled the popcorn ears by hand.

Dad observed his nearly unbroken promise to not work on Sunday, less for religious reasons than for a practical one. Dad's observation was if you couldn't get it done in six days, you either "didn't work hard enough or didn't know what you were doing."

However, even on Sundays, the twice-a-day milking of our twenty-five head of Holstein and Jersey cows still went on. Dad now used two heavy, stainless steel Surge brand suction cup milking machines instead of milking all the cows by hand, squirting the raw milk into a stainless steel pail placed under the cow. His huge, calloused hands represented a lifetime of milking in this manner. While an improvement from hand milking, the machines did not completely end the hard work. The steel machines were heavy, and as a boy I could hardly lift them when they were filled with milk. Milk from the machines then had to be poured into individual steel milk cans, each weighing over one hundred pounds. Dad loaded the cans onto a homemade two-wheeled cart and hauled them to the milk house. Later, a large stainless steel milk holding tank installed in a building by the barn brought an end to the days of hauling cans. After much nagging, Dad finally allowed me to turn the former smoke and milk house into a combination laboratory/clubhouse that, according to the sign I tacked on the door, my brothers were not supposed to enter.

In the winter, the cows stayed inside, and the gutters behind them had to be cleaned every day. Dad pitched the cow manure from the gutters into a wheelbarrow that he pushed along a single one-by-twelve-inch board suspended between the barn door and the top of the manure pile, where he dumped it out. Dad, always protective of his sons, said he would use the wheelbarrow himself, explaining it was too dangerous for us on the long, slippery, wobbly ramp. On weekends, we used pitchforks to toss manure from the pile into a spreader, whose rotating wheels then distributed it around the fields as fertilizer. Hay from the big red barn had to be thrown down from the mow with a pitchfork and carried to the cows at each milking time. We drank raw unpasteurized milk that Dad brought to the house every day from the barn in a large, open, stainless steel pail. The milk had a strong, rich flavor since it had not been pasteurized or separated from the cream.

In the summer, the huge garden east of our house contained tomatoes, string beans, lettuce, and sweet corn but never bell peppers, onions, or squash, which Mom disliked. Instead of growing strawberries, we bought them from Ad Geris who lived on Butler Road, a couple of miles to the west of our farm. The first time Mom asked me to ride my bike to Ad's place by myself to buy strawberries, I experienced another milestone in my life. This was something that my older brothers had done, but I had not. Riding my bike away our farm out of sight of Mom, Dad, and my brothers constituted one more step toward independence and adventure.

I rode west on Zenobia Road past Charlie Leider's place and Francis Nestor's well-kept farm into the setting sun. Ad lived in a small, run-down house, a shack really, set back from Butler Road behind tall, thick weeds and bull thistles. The house was grayish black, never having been painted. Ad lived alone with no visible means of support other than selling strawberries in the summer. Part of the inside of the house had a dirt floor and kerosene lanterns for light. The ghostly look of his house and surroundings as I rode my bike closer made me wonder whether I shouldn't have come alone.

I nervously pounded on his rough-lumber front door and waited. Finally, I heard the metal latch click, the door creak open, and Ad motioned for me to come in. I could smell the strong odor of sweat and urine probably coming from his shabby black clothes, which included a long, scraggly, untucked shirt. To enter the house, you had to step over a huge beam onto a dirt floor. Only the back part of the house had a rough-cut lumber floor. I gave him the exact amount of change that Mom sent with me to pay him for two quarts of strawberries. He asked if I wanted to stay awhile, but I grabbed the paper-thin wooden baskets from his outstretched hands and quickly ran to my bike, placing them in the bike's wire basket. I pedaled home as fast as I could, with berries flying in all directions.

One hot, muggy summer day, while in our garden, Bud, our three-legged fox terrier, bit off most of my lower lip as he jumped up into my face. Although he had never worn a collar, I had tied a rope around his neck that day to lead him around. After bringing me home from the hospital, Mom told Dad, "Austin, get rid of Bud now!" Bud had been a birthday gift to me from Uncle Bob.

"The dog didn't do anything wrong," Dad reminded Mom. He knew I was the one at fault, not the dog. It is easy to blame something or someone else when they can't defend themselves, and easy to stay silent when you know the fault of your own actions is being misplaced somewhere else. We need the inner courage and strength to accept responsibility for the consequences of our own doing. Bud with his three legs—the fourth having been cut off in the sharp triangular teeth of Dad's mowing machine—didn't go anywhere and eventually died of old age.

Constant work was always part of my early life and stayed with me in later years. I often thought about my role in life as the youngest child with three older brothers. I felt I had to prove myself, always trying to keep up with my brothers who knew more about the world than I did. Even today, I want to be doing something, to be useful and productive, and while many see it as work, I don't. Even at an early age, I thought a lot about my surroundings. Although I wanted to travel, explore, and learn more about the rest of the world, I liked my place in it. I felt secure on our nearly self-sufficient farm, which provided our own eggs, milk, meat, vegetables, grapes, apples, popcorn, walnuts, and blackberries. We lived there with little reliance on others, producing almost everything we needed to survive. We were isolated, independent, and loners, really.

No one came by to visit us unless they were asked, and we usually didn't ask anyone. I genuinely enjoyed being alone and still do, even though I had lots of friends from school and the farms around us.

I learned directions at an early age and still orient myself by picturing in my mind the landmarks surrounding our farm. Francis Nestor was our neighbor to the west, at the corner of Butler Road. He always seemed distinguished to me. He wore a gray fedora hat, cotton slacks, and a shirt, unlike Dad and other farmers who wore work caps and bib overalls. I started to wonder about how others looked and dressed. Francis's business-style clothes may have made him appear better educated or more successful at first glance, but as I grew older, I realized the interior of a person was more important than their exterior, even if it looked polished.

I associated north with Dottie Foster and her bachelor brother, Elmer Wing, who lived across Zenobia Road in the Foster place. Both stood under five feet tall with no children and only a cocker spaniel named Laddie for companionship. Dottie bought their first car, a Model T with no gearshift, just pedals with the speed control on the steering wheel. Later Elmer drove a 1932 Ford and sometimes gave us a ride, but he just never learned to shift its gears. We could hear Elmer leave with a loud roar as he drove down Zenobia Road out of sight, still in first gear.

Whenever Dottie and Elmer saw me, they pulled my hair straight up, saying, "You're growing like a weed." They ate boiled dandelion greens pulled from their front yard, something we wouldn't think of doing. Dad's later purchase of the Foster place included about eighty acres, some farm buildings, machinery, and an old streetcar used for grain storage. I started one of my first money-making ventures in that streetcar, when Dad agreed to pay me ten cents for each large grain rat I killed, some of which were the size of a cat.

East was Emil Gemmel's farm and Clarence Draper's place. Clarence, a farmer who also sold fertilizer, drove a maroon-colored Mercury with a back seat full of empty Red Man chewing tobacco bags he tossed there. Emil Gemmel worked for the Ohio State Highway Department, and bad weather meant he got called late at night on our party line that simultaneously rang at our own house. As neighbors, we could listen to each other's calls.

West was Charlie Leider's place. Charlie's daughter, Genevieve, had moved away, but his son, Jay, lived with his wife Fran across Zenobia Road from our farm and to the east of the Foster place. Dad said Fran was "off in the head," never explaining the phrase that he used more than once during his observations of unusual or irrational behavior in others. After Jay had taken away her car keys, and hearing from our house what seemed like hours of screaming and abusive swearing at Jay or whoever was within earshot, Fran drove their Ferguson tractor down Zenobia Road past our house to the Riverside Tavern in Clarksfield Hollow to buy alcohol. On Fran's return trip home on the tractor, she had several six-packs of beer stacked on her lap. There are probably just as many or even more who seem to act irrationally, whether you live in an urban or suburban setting, but the rural life made it stand out more. Jay started raising turkeys and eventually quit farming his land, setting up turkey coops everywhere on his property. He then patched together old, discarded plywood panels from a World War II surplus building to use as a makeshift turkey processing faculty. With the help of the neighbors he hired, including Mom and Dad, they killed, defeathered, and cut up the turkeys. Mom's job was to remove the tiny pin feathers and Dad the big ones. This was hard, messy work done in the midst of the smell from the turkey farm that became intolerable when the wind blew from the east toward our place, which fortunately seldom happened. Later Jay was found dead at his mom's place, and his son Bob committed suicide.

I associated south with the Nickel Plate Railroad line and Karl Langendoufer's place. Karl fought for the Kaiser's army in World War I and lost his left arm in battle. Mom, ignoring the real cause of Karl's injury, told us when we'd hang out the window of our 1939 Ford on a hot summer day, "See what happened to Karl when he kept his arm out the car window? The same thing will happen to you." We didn't really believe Mom, at least once we got older, but the admonition was unusual and memorable, which I'm sure was really Mom's goal.

Also at the southern end of our farm were fifteen acres of woods that felt magical to me. The woods were a getaway from the rest of the world. I loved the little spring-fed pond there. One winter afternoon at this frozen pond, my brothers teased and pestered me to come out on the ice and play hockey with them. I finally did go on the ice and immediately fell and got up and fell two or three more times. The last time I felt sick and complained to my brothers that my left arm hurt. After saying there was nothing wrong with me, they refused to take me back across the fields to the house, so I waited in the cold until they wanted to leave. When I finally got to the house, my left arm had swollen, and Mom had to cut off the sleeve of my winter jacket to undress me. I ended up in the nearby Oberlin hospital to have a cast put on my broken left elbow. Later, after having left the cast on too long, I followed the doctor's suggestion to carry around a pail of rocks at home every day after school with my left arm to help straighten it out.

Even on the brightest summer days, parts of the woods remained dark and shaded by the thick canopy of beech, oak, elm, and hickory trees, as well as sugar maples that would soon turn a gorgeous red with the coming of fall.

We all need a special place to separate ourselves, if only for a brief time, from the surrounding world. This place can be any version of a getaway, a favorite walking path, a friend's house or yard, a park or playground. It is not limited to a magical country setting as I encountered. When you're in the middle of a time or place that overwhelms you, close your eyes and briefly picture in your mind that special place.

While there was beauty and peacefulness on the farm, there was ever-present suffering as well. I saw it all the time but couldn't understand the reason for the constant death and suffering of animals even though I was part of it. Death was everywhere: the shooting of dogs by Dad if they chased sheep, the trapping and killing of animals for their fur that I participated in, a baby lamb or calf born dead, the slaughter of animals for food, the castration of screaming lambs, and the Sunday ritual of chopping off the head of a chicken and watching it die to eat for dinner.

The red fox, coming from its den in our swamp, left a trail of blood and feathers after killing our chickens and frequently all our young ducks. The skunk from the pond behind the house would smash open all the warm eggs from the sitting hen's nest, leaving both the half-grown and the unhatched dead baby chicks scattered everywhere.

By contrast, new life was everywhere on the farm as well. Calves, pigs, and lambs were born, and chicken eggs hatched. Litter after litter of new kittens appeared. Spring brought a glorious rebirth of crops, trees, and plants. When hunters killed a mother fox near our swamp, Dad helped me rescue the baby fox. I kept it in a cage and fed it by hand until it got big enough to live on its own. In one form or another on the farm, we learned about the rhythm of life and death that involved the animals, but later in life I could see it also applied to us as human beings. Ecclesiastes 3 pretty well sums up that rhythm, which may have been more noticeable on our farm because we saw and heard life and death on a constant basis.

Chapter 3

MOVING
TO THE FARM

Beginning in college, I became interested in the history of our farm and surrounding area and began asking questions of Mom and Dad. I learned they first moved to the farm from nearby Brighton in 1936. A few months later in February 1937, Mom gave birth to twins, my older brothers Rolland and Richard, who were born about five years before me.

That move, while only a few miles to their new place on Zenobia Road in adjoining Huron County, had a huge significance in our family's life. Dad, with the help of Uncle Russell (who was married to Mom's sister Lucille), loaded everything they owned on the bed of his hay wagon and hitched it to Russell's old yellow Case tractor. Dad's two work horses, Prince and Bill, and his pony were tied to the back of Uncle Russell's wagon. Pulling the wagon with the horses and pony walking behind, they traveled over rough dirt and gravel roads past "Blue Fly Junction" where Alex Justice had lived, and which was now only a forgotten shack. Justice became a local legend for the clothes of animal hides he stitched together and wore. He slept in his homemade wooden coffin. He liked showing it to his visitors, eventually realizing his long-held wish to be buried in the rough-lumber resting place.

The Zenobia Road farm had been abandoned for years before Dad got there. Owned by George Terwilliger, president of the local Wellington Bank, the farm had been in the Terwilliger family since an ancestor, William Terwilliger, traveled there from New York in the mid-1800s to what was then Indian country. He took over the land that had originally been given to his sisters but never occupied by them. He left the Ohio area as did many others, hoping to find riches and adventure in far-off California, something I would later try for a different kind of success. Terwilliger returned to Ohio to clear the Zenobia Road land and build the original part of the house where we lived many years later. Before Dad got there, a tenant had rented the farm from Terwilliger for several years but didn't make payments or keep up the place. Eventually Terwilliger forced out the tenant, who left behind a mess, including hundreds of empty Prince Albert tobacco tins.

When Dad first arrived at the farm, he found it overgrown with weeds, crab apple trees, and huge bull thistles taller than he was. Only a narrow footpath led through the overgrowth from Zenobia Road to the house and on to the big barn to the south. It took Dad, with the help of Uncle Russell, several months to clear the fields, rebuild the barn, and plant the first crop of potatoes near the swamp. When Dad finished clearing the land, he left one small clump of apple trees near the foundation of what had been a log cabin. The trees, according to local lore, had been planted by John Chapman from seeds grown in his nursery in nearby Mansfield. Chapman, or "Johnny Appleseed," as he became known, had frequented this area of Ohio.

Dad and Mom worked out an unusual agreement with Terwilliger and his wife, Stella. They agreed to pay George and Stella thirty dollars a month for as long as either of them was alive. It was the Great Depression, and Dad and Mom had no money to buy the farm or even make a down payment. George Terwilliger didn't want to deed the farm to a young couple who might not be able to pay. George committed suicide in 1948, but Stella lived to be 103 years old. Every month for forty years, Dad drove to nearby Wellington to visit Stella, a tall, erect lady with yellowish hair pulled tight into a bun at the back of her head. He gave her the thirty-dollar check for the farm and sold her a dozen eggs. After she died, Dad and Mom had to sort out the farm ownership. Terwilliger had put the deed to the farm in a safe deposit box in the Wellington Bank where he served as president, with instructions to give it to Dad when he and his wife were both deceased. By the time Stella died about fifty years later, George, the First Wellington Bank, and the deed were all gone. The ownership of the farm and Dad's rights became an issue after the Terwilliger relatives tried to deny Dad's ownership. Finally, it got resolved in Dad's favor with the help of Ron Freeman, a friend and Ohio attorney I contacted.

Dad was nineteen and Mom just seventeen when they married. Dad first saw Mom when she got off the school bus from Rochester to attend high school at Brighton. Dad recalled that he'd bought an engagement ring while Mom was still in high school. When they did set a date to marry, it was rescheduled because Dad's mother had died. Neither Mom nor Dad ever dated anyone else. As I think back, this was a marvelous little love story that neither I nor most people could replicate. They first lived in the little house of Dad's birth on Ohio State Route 511, just south of Brighton. Mom graduated early from high school, having skipped a grade because of her test scores, and began working in a dry goods store in nearby Wellington, riding the train back and forth every day from her home in nearby Rochester.

At this time, Dad was working on Grandpa Bert Ewell's ferret farm, helping "Pa," as he called him, raise ferrets sold for hunting and laboratory use. At the ferret farm, the animals kept in cages were voracious eaters of a mush-like meal containing chunks of horse meat. One of Dad's jobs was to kill the horses they kept to feed the ferrets by shooting them in the head with a single-shot, 12-gauge shotgun, which I still have. The gun's sight consisted only of a rusty screw at the end of the barrel, but Dad didn't worry about the sight's accuracy since he killed them at close range. Later in life, this experience turned him away from killing anything for sport. He wouldn't go hunting with my brothers and me, saying he "couldn't hit the broadside of a barn," but he never discussed the real reason.

My brothers and I often went raccoon hunting. My brother Dan bought a bluetick coonhound dog through a mail-order catalog, and it came shipped in a crate by railroad from Alabama to Ohio. This breed of dog was known for its faultless raccoon tracking, but Dan's bluetick would barely run and stayed in its cage shaking from what appeared to be fear. We had several other "coon dogs" that were skinny, ran fast, and were the opposite of Dan's bluetick. You could hear dogs trained to track raccoons changing the sound and tone of their bark, which signaled how close they were to "treeing" the animal, forcing it to scamper up a tree for safety. The best nights for hunting were cold and misty when the dogs could track the scent of their prey. Our goal wasn't really to catch and kill a raccoon; it was a time for us siblings to be together. The smell of the kerosene lanterns on those cold, damp nights in the woods and the sound of the howling dogs in the distance are still clear in my mind.

My siblings and I were busy year-round with hard work, and we didn't know about the tensions in Dad's family. Dad's older brother, Clark, had become partners with Pa, and in 1926 they formed Bert Ewell & Son Grain Elevator, located on the south side of the Nickel Plate Railroad crossing in Brighton. They sold livestock feed and bought grain from neighboring farmers.

In 1946 when Pa died, the business name was changed to Clark Ewell & Son, a business between Clark and his son Ray, Dad's nephew. The family never discussed the hard feelings caused by the business partnership between Pa and Clark and the exclusion of the other siblings, but we kids had heard just enough to realize that something was wrong in their relationship. Even later in life, Dad only spoke about the matter one time. "I have only been sued once in life," he said, "and that was by my brother." Clark's suit against Dad, over a disputed bill at Bert Ewell & Son Grain Elevator, never left Dad's memory. Mom, direct as always in her observations, put it another way, saying after Grandpa Bert's death, "Uncle Clark got the business, and we got the funeral bills."

I was very young at the time and never once recall seeing Grandpa Bert, even though he lived only three miles from our farm. I have a picture of him wearing what appeared to be a crooked toupee, as an unknown disease had caused him to lose all his hair, including his eyebrows and eyelashes. Grandma Minnie Tucker Ewell, Dad's mother, died before I was born. Sometime after Minnie's death, Grandpa Bert met and married a woman named Isabell, whom he left a widow when he died in 1946 at age seventy-four; she was fifty-eight. No one ever mentioned her name, or that Grandpa Bert had remarried, or what happened to Isabell Ewell after Pa's death. I only learned about her many years later after Mom and Dad had passed away. Grandpa's remarriage to Isabell and his business dealings with Uncle Clark pretty much soured his relationship with Dad and our family. I found this information by chance in a one-page document in Dad's old papers that I had shipped to California after his death. The document was signed by all five of Pa's children and documented Clark's purchase of all interest his four siblings may have had in the Bert Ewell & Son Grain Elevator business with Pa, upon payment by Clark of $700 to each of his four siblings. The document also mentioned that Clark had already acquired any interest held by Isabell.

Once when I was home on summer break from law school, Dad told me he was going to see Clark. "Why don't you ride along with me?" he suggested. We made our way to Clark's house, and Dad knocked on the door as I stood nearby. Clark came to the door to greet Dad but did not invite him in. They spoke only a few words that I could not hear. I'll never know what was said, but Dad told me on the way home, "It was something I had to do."

Uncle Johnny, another of Dad's brothers, lived on a farm at the top of a high hill on State Route 511 between Brighton and Rochester. His daughter, Judy, attended school with me throughout elementary and high school grades along with her brother, Leonard, who was a couple grades ahead of me. We never got together with Uncle Johnny's family either. Dad had another brother, Paul, whom I never met. I learned later he lived only a few miles to the southwest of us, near New London. Years later after I left Ohio, I learned Paul had six children whose names all curiously began with the letter B, first cousins whom I had never met. Dad never mentioned Paul, and I knew of him only when I asked about the identity of a young boy in dad's family portrait. Dad had one sister, Olive, who married a man named George and lived on Route 511 South, not far from the Brighton Congregational Church. Dad's relationship with Olive seemed better than with his brothers. In the end, the plots of Grandpa Bert, Grandma Minnie, and Dad's brothers Clark and Johnny, along with his sister, Olive, were on the south side of the Brighton Cemetery, separated by a gravel driveway and a stone monument from the final resting place of Mom, Dad, and my sister, Betty, on the opposite side of the same cemetery. When I'm asked about my family, it's hard for others to understand all five members of Dad's generation living within three or four miles of each other and having no contact. All families have tension and strife, but some is more widely known about. The degree of strife is not as important as how we react to it. In this current age, everything and everyone is subject to social media exposure, the opposite of a time and place in a Midwest farm community when there were still things called secrets.

The carved stone monument separating our family in death in the cemetery depicts the three Revolutionary War fighters in the painting *Spirit of '76* who had lived in the Brighton area. This threesome, the Brighton Fife and Drum Corps, usually joked around, but for the purposes of this painting, they were depicted as solemn soldiers.

Mom's family lived a few miles south of Brighton on State Route 511 in the small town of Rochester. We got together often with Mom's sister, Aunt Lucille, or "Annyceil" as we pronounced it growing up, and Mom's brother, Uncle Bob. Mom's other brother, Dean, a railroad executive who lived in Cleveland, had two children, my cousins Scott and Karen. We didn't travel to see Uncle Dean very often, and when we did, he seemed distant to me. Grandpa Eli Thompson, Mom's dad, originally from Illinois, worked as a mail sorter on the railroad and eventually went west to Kansas where he met and married his wife, Estelle Biddinger, my Grandma "Nettie." He taught at the Kansas Normal School in Pratt, Kansas, the predecessor of today's community college. Estelle's parents homesteaded prairie land in Kansas where they first lived in a house made of sod. I learned later that Estelle's parents didn't want her to marry Eli, considering him a tall, mustached ladies' man who might be trouble, and rumor had it that he did cause some trouble of an unknown nature. Dad said Eli was smart and always tinkered around but never worked very hard. On the rare occasions I saw him, he was usually eating a bowl of bread and milk. He spent time experimenting with things. "He even tried to grow peanuts," Dad said. "Now, anybody with enough sense to get out of the rain knows you don't grow peanuts in Ohio."

My only recollection of Grandpa Eli was during a visit as a boy to Grandma's house. He lay on what turned out to be his deathbed in Grandma's parlor. This room, kept dark with heavy drawn curtains on the windows, had a print on one wall that fascinated me. Jean François Millet's *The Gleaners* pictured three stooped women gathering leftover grain from a harvested field in a colorless surrounding behind heavy beveled glass. The painting was so simple with only soft muted colors of the grainfield and the gleaners. I thought it portrayed the timeless work of the farm and harvest and the importance of even a few tiny kernels of grain to most of the world. We are finally coming to realize that it is important to salvage and reuse things that have been discarded, even the smallest of grains left in a harvested field.

Mom was born in Kansas City, Kansas, before Eli and Nettie returned to Ohio. She loved adventure and didn't fit the mold of local farm wives. She learned to play golf and traveled to Europe and the Holy Land. She loved music and became the pianist at the local church we attended. Her love of books became an obsession, as she read two or three at the same time, switching back and forth between the hundreds of volumes we had in the house, both on shelves and put away in boxes. Early on and through Mom's influence, I developed an interest in books of all kinds. She often took me to the Herrick Memorial Library in nearby Wellington, a solid redbrick building with dark mahogany furniture and bookshelves. While I was still in college, Mom attended night classes at Kent State University hoping to become a schoolteacher as her sister Lucille had done after high school. She usually arrived home after midnight, having driven over two hours each way for the university classes. In 1962, I watched from the audience as Mom, at the age of fifty-two, graduated from Kent State summa cum laude.

Dad never went to college or traveled outside the United States. "If I want to see foreigners, I'll go to Cleveland," he would say, but he still encouraged Mom to continue her education and her travels. I think Dad wanted Mom, and later us kids, to experience things he must have thought about but never did himself.

Dad encouraged his children to leave home. I wanted to leave someday, but I didn't express my thoughts to Dad for concern that I would hurt his feelings. Having a son was a farmer's dream come true, and Dad had four of them.

I mentioned to him one day while we took a break from the summer heat in the shade of a nearby tree, "Dad, I'll be going out to California after I graduate from college."

"I know, son," he said. "I'm so proud of you."

I replied, "But I like it on the farm, and if you need my help, I could stay rather than go to law school."

Looking at me, Dad said, "I'll miss you, but son, this is no life for you." I thought, *He's not just talking about hard work; he wants me to take the opportunity to go out into the world for adventure and, hopefully, success.*

When I did leave the farm, I started to look back at the beauty and history of our life and surroundings on Zenobia Road. Over the years, I took pictures of each of the four seasons of our farm and recorded their unique beauty. As I studied the photos, I began to see and appreciate more and more the timeless beauty that was right there in our own backyard.

The animals, plants, and beauty of the area remained the same over the years. The area had changed very little during all the centuries before 1936 when our family first occupied the land.

Charles II of England deeded this and other lands to his brother, the Duke of York, and even then, I'm sure, the muskrats were building their houses in the swamp at the back of our farm.

When the states of New York, Virginia, Massachusetts, and Connecticut gave up their claims to this land, and the colonies acknowledged their allegiance to the federal government, I am sure the raccoons were already coming to the little spring-fed pond in our woods.

When General "Mad" Anthony Wayne met the enemy at the Battle of Fallen Timbers and killed nearly every Wyandot chief in northwest Ohio, the deer that ate the blackberries on the bushes next to the woods had already been there for hundreds of years. The hickory nuts gathered up by the red squirrels in the woods and the bright red maple leaves of fall meant winter would soon be there. The quiet blanket of snow over the pasture and leafless trees in the woods happened every winter. The dark green stain from the black walnuts in the pasture, the bitter crab apples, and the poisonous red berry bushes had always been there. The new lush green leaves of the beech and maple trees and the giant elm appeared every spring.

I wanted to know the history of our farm before 1936, and that led me to research the background of the area around Clarksfield and eastern Huron County. In contrast to the tranquil natural beauty of the area, the human history there had begun with violence and suffering. There were Indian battles and killings. Seneca John of the Wyandot Indians was killed by his brothers, and Jim Organtz by his son. I later understood that the suffering I saw in my youth on our farm, the constant slaughter of animals and castrating of lambs, was a continuation of its history. Later, the tragic and violent death of my brother Dale and his family continued the cycle.

I found out the "Sufferer's Lands" as our area was known, referred to property that was given to the inhabitants of Danbury, Connecticut, who had suffered and been killed and whose homes had been burned by the British Army. The recorded written history of our farm's ownership began on the afternoon of April 26,

1777. On that day, about two thousand British troops destroyed the town of Danbury. After several years of meetings and promises, the Connecticut State Legislature agreed to compensate those Connecticut residents who had suffered the loss of their property at the hands of the British in the Revolutionary War.

The legislature voted to deed about 500,000 acres of land in an area known as the Western Reserve Indian Territory to benefit residents of Danbury and other Connecticut towns. This land later became two Ohio counties, Huron and Erie. The people who received the land were known as Sufferers. The uninhabited land given out by the Connecticut legislature was later surveyed and divided into townships, sections, and lots and became known as the Firelands.

According to the history of the area, the Sufferers and their descendants eventually held a lottery where each drew a slip of paper entitling them to a particular lot in the Western Reserve Firelands area. The records show that one of the Reserve Sufferers, Ezra Dibble, ended up with a thousand acres, including the area that would one day become our 160-acre farm.

Before Dibble could move to the land, Indian claims to the area had to be settled. According to historical records, the area around our farm was considered Indian hunting grounds.

The Indians did not buy and sell land as Dibble and those of us who came later would do; they believed land could be used but never owned by them. It was inconceivable to the Indians that pieces of paper could give one person the right to the land and another the obligation to leave that land. Regardless, the piece of paper that Dibble ended up with during the lottery made him the first "owner" of our farm under the Sufferers' system of land ownership. Later, in 1817, the first descendants of the Sufferers came to our area and named it Clarksfield after James Clark, one of those settlers.

Even with the passage of time and the succession of future owners, the beauty of the land itself remained the same. It was my awareness and appreciation for the beauty that changed. I could never be or think the same after growing up on the little farm on Zenobia Road. I changed as a person, and while it happened slowly over a period of time, it did forever affect the appreciation I had later in life for the environment we live in. I traveled to many states and foreign countries, but I kept in mind the beauty of the four seasons on our farm. My appreciation for the beauty and history of our own farm helped me understand that I was different from most farm boys who didn't seem to share my feelings.

Chapter 4

LEAVING
THE FARM

As I grew up, familiar routines marked our days and the seasons of the year. In winter before dawn, I could hear Dad down in the basement banging on the inside of the steel furnace box with an iron poker trying to break up the clinkers. The iron hitting against the steel shook the walls of the house. By then, I was thirteen years old and used to this kind of sound, as our only heat came from a coal and wood furnace in the basement. To me this place was dark, damp, and mysterious. Divided into two separate rooms, our basement's only access was by sandstone slab steps leading down from the washroom.

Dad had cut holes in the floors of the dining room above the furnace box and of the second story bedrooms and placed metal grates in the holes so heat from the furnace would rise up through the grates to warm the upper floors. Before going to bed, he built up the fire with large chunks of wood and big lumps of jet-black coal, hoping it would burn all night, but by early morning, it was generally out.

Winter mornings in northeastern Ohio often meant temperatures below freezing and sometimes as low as zero. We lived about twenty miles south of Lake Erie, and the Canadian border

63

was only thirty miles farther. As kids, we stayed in bed on most cold mornings and waited for Dad to get the fire restarted, except for Christmas, the only day of the year we got out of bed earlier.

On winter mornings during school, we got out of bed before the fire was warm enough to heat the whole house. "Austin, quit banging around down there!" Mom would yell to Dad through the grate to the basement. "Get the fire going; the boys need to get to school."

On school mornings, there was chaos with five kids trying to get ready at the same time without a bathroom or running water. Our water came from a red cast-iron hand pump at the kitchen sink whose source was a cistern in the washroom floor. A lather of Lava brand soap and a splash of ice-cold water to our face was followed by brushing our teeth with baking soda, salt, and later toothpaste. This was about the extent of our personal hygiene during the week. Our once-a-week bath took place on Saturday nights.

Getting dressed for school on those winter days took time. We wore long underwear with the button-up flap in back and buttoned-up hole in front, wool shirts, and long knee-length socks. There was no lingering in the bathroom because we didn't have one, and no one considered going to the outhouse in freezing weather. We used a pot kept in the house as a place to relieve ourselves in the winter. On most school days, Dad let us skip morning chores and do the work when we got home, but he had to milk the cows every morning and night, 365 days a year.

Dad tried to get back to the house from the barn before we left for school so he could eat breakfast with us. Most men I saw in those days who worked with their hands and backs ate a big breakfast of bacon, eggs, and potatoes. Dad might have been ahead of his time when it came to nutrition, as he ate oatmeal almost every morning.

We needed to be ready to leave for school before Floyd Eaton blew the horn on the Brighton school bus as he headed east down Zenobia Road. His two sons went to school with us and rode in the bus with him. Floyd would start honking his horn when he passed Charlie Leider's place heading toward our farm.

We were supposed to go to school in the New London School District in Huron County and not the Brighton School District in neighboring Lorain County, although we considered Brighton our hometown. We never went to the town of New London, which was small and seemed backward, with no connection to our family. Mom told Dad she didn't want us to go to school there. There was only one coffee shop restaurant in New London. Dad and I ate there one night while Mom was taking classes. Dad ordered fish and couldn't eat it but said he would take it home for the cat. The next morning he told me, "You know the fish is bad when the cat won't eat it."

Mom wouldn't give up on her idea, telling Dad, "Austin, do something about the school district. The kids won't amount to a hill of beans at New London."

Dad mentioned to a member of the New London School Board of Trustees he knew that he wanted his kids to go to school in Brighton, where he himself had attended school. He convinced the school board to devise a plan to change the school district boundary rules, something that was unheard of at the time and might still be today. Dad and the board came up with a unique solution. The school board adopted a rule that if you lived on the north side of Zenobia Road you would go to school in New London, and if you lived on the south side, you would go to school in Brighton. There were only two houses on the south side of the road, ours and Charlie Leider's. Charlie was old, and his kids had long since moved away. So the result of Dad's political efforts meant the new boundary arrangement applied only to us. Even though Dad's education ended at high school, over the years I came to recognize and appreciate just how effective he could be. I learned from his nonconfrontational approach and his ability to change people's minds on positions and practiced it later in life myself, often with success.

His talent continued to be useful. Years later, Dad got a traffic ticket from the Ohio State Highway Patrol that could have cost him a huge fine and his driver's license, which at his age would mean he could never drive again. He was charged with making a left turn without signaling and causing a large tractor trailer approaching him from behind to veer off the highway and crash. I called Dad from California and suggested I hire an Ohio lawyer to help him. He refused.

"I've been driving for almost fifty years and never had a ticket."

"But, Dad," I said, "I checked with the court, and the truck driver is represented by the Ohio Trucking Association's attorney."

"Well, what difference does that make?" he asked.

"I'm sure it will make a difference," I said.

"I don't think so; I'll just tell it the way it happened. I turned on my left blinker to turn into the Congregational church driveway from State Route Eighteen. I moved the turn signal with my right hand over the steering wheel because I have arthritis in my left and it bothers me to move it much. That guy was just going too fast in the tractor trailer and couldn't stop; that's why he almost rear-ended me and went off the road, and that's all there is to it," Dad said.

"But the highway patrol's report said the truck driver gave a statement that you didn't signal."

"Well, that's because the trucking association is probably cozy with the highway patrol."

Dad went to court on the traffic case without a lawyer and proved he didn't need one. The judge listened to Dad's story, along with the testimony of the trucker, the highway patrol officer, and the attorney for the Ohio Trucking Association out of Columbus. He then dismissed the case against Dad.

My first very small step toward leaving the farm involved getting on the bus to ride to school at Brighton, which meant leaving the security of our farm to travel about four miles. I had never been away from home except to church at Brighton, to Aunt Lucille's house in nearby Rochester, and to a couple of the stores in Wellington. The Brighton school had been built in the 1920s and seemed secure and self-contained, like our farm. In 1926, Dad, as president of his little class, had graduated from high school in this same white stucco-and-brick, single-story building with his seven classmates. All twelve grades still met in the same building when I got there. Since kindergarten did not exist in the 1940s, I started school in Miss Hardy's first grade class.

The main entrance to the school was set back from State Route 18 with a gravel entry between the highway and the front door. Just inside the entrance to the left of the double front doors, the library occupied a small, compact, solid-looking room with floor-to-ceiling wooden bookshelves. On the opposite side of the entrance was the science lab, which fascinated me with its glass beakers, bottles of chemicals, and pungent odors from student experiments gone wrong. Straight ahead from the entrance was the gym, surrounded by windows with a stage and heavy black curtains.

Miss Hardy's first and second grade and Mrs. Rosero's third and fourth grade classes were to the left of the entrance. To the right of the entrance was Miss Crandall's combined fifth and sixth grades and Mrs. Livermore's seventh and eighth grade classes. My class had seventeen students including me, and the other grades were about the same. As the youngest sibling and the last to start school, I had a lot of thoughts about where—or even if—I would fit in. Betty, the oldest of us, was already preparing to leave for college. She substituted one day as a teacher in my first grade class, and when I started to act up a little, she reprimanded me, and that ended the matter. I really didn't want to do anything wrong or cause trouble that day and hoped no one else would. My oldest brother, Dale, was a good athlete who excelled at both basketball and baseball, and I thought I could never achieve his athletic and social prowess. Dale mentioned to Mom one day at the beginning of the basketball season, "Alice would like to have Ben wear a cowboy uniform and be the Rangers' team mascot." Alice was Dale's girlfriend and the head cheerleader, and Mom liked her.

Mom said, "It's okay with me if your little brother doesn't mind." I don't recall being asked if I minded, but Alice helped me get over my stage fright, and I have fond memories of my role as mascot. I posed for a picture with the team members including Dale towering over me. I liked being Dale's little brother at school. Everyone seemed to like and admire him. I was Dan and Dick's little brother too, but that was different. They made fun of my glasses, something Dale would never have done. Dan and Dick were closer in age to me but seemed so much surer of themselves, Dan with his athletic abilities and Dick with his social skills. At home, we all seemed alike, having kidded around and hassled each other on an equal basis, but at school I started to see the difference in personalities, abilities, and approach of my siblings that I didn't recognize at home. I began to see that people, even your own family, can act differently in different settings.

▶ THE NEIGHBORHOOD

My best grade school friend at Brighton was Gary Barnes, or "Bugs," as we called him. He lived to the west of Brighton on Route 18, between Blue Fly Junction and White Fox Corners, a crossroads with only a couple of shacks remaining that bore the name of the albino fox reportedly once seen there. Gary's dad, Wendell, worked at the Thew Shovel Company in Lorain that made heavy construction equipment. I noticed Wendell's eyes had dark circles under them. I saw this in other factory workers including my uncle Bob and experienced it myself later during my summer job at the Bendix-Westinghouse factory. I began to think about two distinct groups of people living in our neighborhood. The farmers had suntans that, before the days of sunscreen, got darker as the summer progressed, and they appeared to be healthier and more energetic. The other group, including Wendell and Uncle Bob, were factory workers exposed to oil, noise, and polluted factory air, all with colorless complexions who appeared less healthy. I also formed the opinion that factory workers doing the same task all day, every day, had a reason to be less happy. On nights and weekends, Wendell tinkered in a shop next to their house, sharpening axes and saws and welding broken farm equipment that Dad and others brought to him.

On one visit, Dad saw a homemade motorbike that Wendell had made for his son and asked him if he could make one for me. He started with a regular bicycle and replaced the back wheel with a small, wide tire. He then welded a little steel platform to the bicycle frame to hold a small gasoline-powered, Briggs & Stratton lawn mower engine. The engine was loud and powerful and was engaged by pulling a starter rope. A V-belt, when tightened by pushing down on a lever near the pedals, turned the back wheel. The contraption had no gears, just stop and go, and the going was very fast. It had a regular bicycle seat and brakes. After starting the engine, I would push down the lever to engage the V-drive belt to the pulley on the engine and take off down the road. I had no helmet, pads, or protection of any kind. Every dog I encountered threatened to make me a potential crash victim. The only way to stop was by releasing the V-belt. I rode the homemade motorbike for miles on the back roads near our farm and was able to experience the freedom of getting away from home long before I drove a car. This newfound freedom became another step in moving away from the security of our farm. Any form of independent transportation can bring freedom. It can be a bike, a scooter, or a pedal car. We feel different about ourselves and our surroundings when we can move on something other than our feet; we feel more in control of our lives.

On the farm we were isolated, self-sufficient, and protected from the outside world. Still, Dad allowed and even encouraged us to take physical risks. The homemade motorbike was only one example of a potentially dangerous toy Dad didn't discourage us from using. For my brothers, Dad bought a cut-down truck with a windshield, frame, and seats, but no enclosed cab. My brothers drove "the jalopy," as we called it, all over the area before they ever had driver's licenses. Besides having dangerous fun with the jalopy, we used it to pull the grain wagon of soybeans or wheat to the Clarksfield Grain Elevator to be sold. It got a real test one hot, humid August night in our woods when Dan, Richard, and I decided to sleep there overnight.

The day had cooled, and the sun was setting behind Charlie Leider's barn. Frogs and crickets were singing for all who would listen. The magnificent maples, birch, and elms of our woods wore their finest summer green. Ferns and numerous ground plants crept right to the bank of the little spring-fed pond where we intended to sleep. The view from our makeshift bed of old blankets next to the pond changed as the surrounding shadows and blackness gave way to the movement of fox, raccoons, and deer that came to the pond for water. All the creatures of the night spoke their own special language, including the owl's eerie sound. The crows and blue jays, always jabbering back and forth during the day, went silent. The possum, nearly blind in daylight, began its nightly outing, and the fox left its den on the hunt for chickens or ducks to kill. With Dan and Richard, I thought our first night alone in the woods would be only one of many to come.

We settled into our place near the pond as a full moon came up over Emil Gemmil's farm. Our talking stopped, and we drifted into sleep. Later, thinking it was a dream, I heard limbs and twigs breaking and saw something coming toward us dressed in white. By then, we were awake and yelling. As we jumped up from the ground, the white-clad creature quickly moved away and let out a loud howl.

"Did you guys hear that?" Richard asked nervously.

Both Dan and I replied almost in a whisper, "I heard something too."

Dan said, "I'm going to start the jalopy and get out of here." Before he finished the sentence, the loud sound of the old truck started, filling the peaceful woods with noise.

"Hey, Dan, wait up!" I said.

Dan was already underway as Richard and I jumped in. We raced down the lane from the woods toward the house, not stopping to open the wooden gate in the lane that splintered in all directions as he drove through it. Out of breath, we ran into the house, woke up Mom and Dad, and tried to explain what we had seen in the woods. We ran upstairs to tell our brother Dale, who seemed to be in bed asleep, but also appeared to be hot and sweaty. Still short of breath from the incident, Richard said, "Dale, you won't believe what we saw in the woods!"

Dale said, "I don't know what you guys are talking about," and rolled over with little interest in our story of the ghostly vision.

Because of the security of our farm life, I didn't really experience fear except that night in the woods that still remains vividly in my mind. Was it caused by some unknown creature in the woods that night, or our oldest brother playing a trick? Could there be an explanation for what we saw that night? I would never know for sure. We all experience fear of the unknown. It is how we deal with this fear that determines the impact it will have on us. We need to show concern about the unknown but not panic. Once we learn to manage our feelings, we will be ready to confront the next unknown that we experience.

Evidence of risks we were allowed to take came in other forms, including the many cars that Dan wrecked during his teenage years, and that Dad replaced. Maybe it was Mom and Dad's way of showing us a way out of our sheltered, secure life on the farm and the little school in Brighton without really discussing that goal with us.

During our teen years around Halloween time, some friends and I became downright destructive. Bob Greenbank, a school friend, came by the farm, and I asked Dad for some pliers and baling wire. This wasn't something a teenager needed at night. Dad didn't say, "No, don't do this." Instead, he said, "I'm not sure what you're doing, but be careful." Bob and I went around to different farms to find an unlocked vehicle so we could tie down the horn and take off running back to our car. The horn would still be blaring long after we had left the scene. The crowning achievement of our destructive acts was wiring the back bumper of a car to a nearby tree or post. We could only imagine what happened the next day when the driver took off, leaving his bumper behind.

A hilarious and nearly deadly incident involved Dan driving us around our fields in one of his cars hunting for pheasants and rabbits with shotguns. Dan suggested, "Why don't you ride on one fender and [his friend] Russ on the other? That way, you'll have a direct shot at the birds." So we did. When Dan stopped the car, Russ and I jumped off, and as we got back into the car, my shotgun discharged, blowing a hole in the car's roof and narrowly missing Dan's head. This brought to mind the reality of the danger that we face in our day-to-day lives and how quickly our lives can change. This time the danger was of our own making. Danger in our lives can and often does occur without warning. The event can be accidental, as it was the day of our hunting, or intentional when many thousands die each year from guns, as was the case of my brother Dale and his family. Yes, we have a right to bear arms, but that does not give us the right to shoot and kill others.

A Brighton school classmate and friend of mine with reddish hair was named Dennis Searles, and called "Redhead," to his chagrin. He lived on a farm on Peck-Wadsworth Road across from the Mosher place. Elon, Redhead's dad, farmed, raised hogs, and bought and sold used farm equipment that Dad described as "junk." He sold Dad a hay wagon in exchange for seven dollars cash and Mom's cast-iron dinner bell that she really wanted to keep. Known as a Herrick bell, it had been cast and sold by the family of the same name, which included Myron Herrick, a former teacher at Brighton school who later became governor of Ohio and ambassador to France.

As soon as Dad got the hay wagon home, one tire went flat and a second one fell off at the hub. Dad seldom got taken advantage of, but this time he had been, and he knew it. Mom constantly reminded him, "Austin, you made a bad deal. You gave away my dinner bell." She was not going to let him forget the transaction. The dinner bell had hung from the corner of our side porch for years, and Mom rang it to call us to meals.

Elon was always offering advice to others.

"You know what happened to the school kids?" he asked me one time while I was visiting his son.

"No, what happened?" I asked.

"Well, they all used to walk two or three miles to school, and that's how they got their exercise. Then the school bought a kid bus and hauled them all back and forth to school, so they got no exercise."

He went on, "Then they had to build a gym for them to run around in and get exercise."

"Okay," I said, but I remembered his point later in life about the unintended consequences of progress. Sometimes the simplest of statements from a random source can stay with you. This was just such a time. Kids riding a bus to school seemed at the time to be progress; only later was there an appreciation for the benefit of walking.

Other neighbors included Ralph Reed, a college graduate, and his wife, Eva, who lived on Route 5 in a house covered in reddish tar paper with chickens running around inside. Dad would remark, "I can't believe he went to college!" We know, of course, that higher education, while sought after, doesn't always have the expected results.

I liked to hear Dad's stories about other neighbors like George Davidson, who vowed he would never cut his beard if his wife bobbed her hair. She never grew her hair long again, and George never cut his beard. He traveled to various farms including ours with his grain thrasher. I would peek around the corner of our barn to look at him. I began to understand how we could see others who look or act different and form opinions about them that may bear no relation to who they really are.

After a doctor prescribed the wrong medicine to Elon for some illness, he eventually lost his eyesight. Years later, they found Elon outside, dead. Redhead never said what happened, and I didn't press him for the answer.

In 1954, my attendance at Brighton school ended at the eighth grade. Because of school district consolidation, I would attend high school in the larger Wellington district about five or six miles away. The move to Wellington, after my sister, Betty, and older brother Dale had graduated from Brighton, was another step toward my desire to leave home for new experiences. Wellington, though it had a population of less than three thousand at the time, was still completely different from Brighton or our farm. To me it was a place of mystery and adventure. There was a town hall, a below-ground pool hall named Paul's, the Lonet single-screen movie theater, taverns, alleyways, and an ice cream parlor called the Dairy Bar. You could order thick milkshakes and hamburgers at the Diner, a converted streetcar near the railroad tracks. Looking back now, it seemed the ideal place to be a teenager in the 1950s.

Now, instead of sixteen classmates, I had about seventy. I was shy but adventurous, wore glasses, and in my freshman year played in the Wellington High School marching band, for which I endured a lot of taunting and verbal abuse from my brothers Dan and Richard, especially Dan, who referred to me as "four eyes."

Mom encouraged me to play the clarinet, the same musical instrument Betty had played very well and Richard tolerably well. In a small school like Brighton, a boy playing the clarinet was looked on with a lot more favor than in a larger school like Wellington. My brothers made fun of me, so I told Mom I wanted to quit the band. After all, the bushy-haired, round-faced Brighton music teacher, Mr. Gantley, told me during one of my lessons in the school's basement boiler room, "You're probably the worst clarinet student I've ever had." His statement really didn't bother me because I agreed with him, and nobody else heard him. In today's era of political correctness, he would probably be fired. Nevertheless, I continued playing the clarinet my freshman year at Wellington High, but even with a new music teacher and more lessons that Mom thought might help, there was little improvement. By the end of my freshman year, both Mom and I realized I couldn't march and play the clarinet at the same time, and that Mr. Gantley had been right. I quit the Wellington High marching band. This is an example of where my parents' encouragement came face-to-face with my lack of ability. Sometimes, with encouragement and effort, we can accomplish things we or others don't think we have the ability to do—and sometimes we can't.

The end of my marching band career coincided with my increased interest in girls and good times, as I wanted to be more like my brothers Dan and Richard. They hung around with a crowd that had parties and belonged to the "Kustom Kats" car club. They wore black corduroy jackets with yellow lettering. They often stayed out late at night and got in fights with Mom and Dad when they finally did come home. From my bedroom I could hear them arguing with Dad. A couple of times the sheriff came to the house, once to tell Mom and Dad about an automobile accident involving Dan, and again when he was involved in a fight that broke the large window of a car dealership. Dan's lifestyle bothered me, not because I thought it was wrong, but because I was concerned about his safety and Mom and Dad's worrying. Later in life I would question Dan about his antics, but at an early age, I didn't feel I had the place to do so.

At the time, eighteen-year-olds could buy low-alcohol content or 3.2 beer in Ohio. Even before then, I had a poorly made fake ID card that said I was eighteen. I began to drink alcohol, something I had never done before. Along with other classmates, I went to parties at the nearby home of a large Italian family that often ended up with a lot of people sick on sloe gin, a sweet, sticky red drink made from sloe berries that produced the worst tipsiness and even worse hangovers. I drank partly to show off to my classmates and partly because I had an ongoing curiosity about doing things I shouldn't—something we tend to carry with us in life. During some school days, I skipped class and went with friends to our classmate Norm Bigelow's house across from the school.

Norm would open up the bottles from his mom's liquor cabinet, and we'd spend the rest of the day talking and drinking.

Mom knew I had started to drink when she began to smell alcohol on my breath at night. "Don't ever let Dad know you've been drinking because of what he's been through," she warned me. I knew that Dad and Mom had never once tasted alcohol, and I'd heard rumors about Dad's father, Grandpa Bert, and his drinking.

The mid- to late-1950s was also a time of cultural change, even in small towns like Wellington. My brother Richard let me use his first 45 rpm phonograph and records from Sun Records in Memphis, Tennessee. Before that I had only heard the 78 rpm Enrico Caruso records that Mom played on our Victrola. Before long, we bought more records like Fats Domino and Bo Diddley. We learned to dance rock 'n' roll at parties where boys slicked their hair back in a ducktail style, turned up their shirt collars, and rolled up their T-shirt sleeves. Our school officers weren't always a match for some of the more unruly students.

Roy McGinnis, the Wellington High School principal, was known by all the students as "Skinhead." He was tall, deep voiced, and bald-headed. School shenanigans in those days could be extreme, and so could the punishment. In Dan and Richard's class, the industrial arts students told the story of holding their teacher, Homer Boudreau, a short, balding man with metal-rimmed glasses, up to the band saw in the shop classroom and cutting the heels off his shoes while he was still wearing them. Another teacher was pushed out of the first-floor study hall window to the ground below. The punishment for these acts consisted of multiple blistering whacks with a large wooden paddle, administered by McGinnis. He purposefully left his office door open so the sound of the paddle and the student's screams could be heard in most areas of the school as an ounce of prevention for others and additional humiliation for the student. There were no parent conferences or lawsuits over severe punishment. This exemplified the adage of the time: "Spare the rod and spoil the child."

I never got in serious trouble and instead became the class jokester. On a bus trip to Cleveland, I really honed my prankster skills. Our entire class and chaperones went to a restaurant that served fish, something we never ate at home. Mom didn't like the smell or taste of fish or lamb, and she never served either one.

I ordered a Lake Erie perch that day in the Cleveland restaurant, served with its head intact and its eyes peering at me. Without anyone seeing me, I cut off the head and stuck it in my pocket. Then I announced, "I thought you were supposed to eat the head." This resulted first in disbelief by my classmates and chaperones and then laughter by the fellow students and concern by the chaperones. While not a very sophisticated performance, I enjoyed the timing and the feeling of getting attention from others.

▶ LEAVING FOR COLLEGE

By my senior year of high school, I had begun making plans for college. By then, my sister and brothers had already left home. My three brothers had each attended Miami University in Oxford, Ohio, and I wanted to follow in their footsteps. At Miami I met, for the first time, kids from families who had a lot of money. My freshman roommate, Frederick Arlington Beaton IV, called "Chick," was the son of the president of a large national corporation. He never studied much or worked very hard.

For Easter break that freshman year, Chick asked me to ride along with him to Daytona Beach, Florida. Chick's parents had given him a brand-new Ford Thunderbird to drive on the trip south. I asked Mom and Dad if I could go and, encouraging my independence as usual, they said yes. We drove from Miami

University in southern Ohio down through Kentucky, Tennessee, Georgia, and the Carolinas into Florida. Before this trip, I had never been out of Ohio, except to Arkansas with Mom and Dad to visit my sister, Betty. Even through several years had passed since the Arkansas trip, segregation and prejudice were still widespread in the South. Bathrooms, restaurants, and drinking fountains were marked either "Whites Only" or "Colored." It was something I hadn't seen before and couldn't understand why people who promoted and supported this ugly custom didn't seem to feel bad about what they were doing.

I experienced a lot of things that differed from life on the farm. Chick's parents had rented us a room in a very nice hotel right on the beach with a sliding glass door, deck, and stunning view of the Atlantic Ocean. There were other college kids there and also some adult tourists. At the beginning of our stay, I ran into an older woman in the hotel lobby who was probably in her midforties. She wore a see-through cover-up over a bikini and seemed to be by herself. "Are you here on college break?" she asked as we waited for the elevator.

"Yes, I go to Miami University in Ohio," I said.

"How did you end up in this hotel?" she asked, and added, "Seems kind of nice for a college student."

I said, "My roommate is paying for everything."

She replied, "Well, good for you."

I said, "How about you?"

She told me that she liked to visit a few times a year. "I like to visit when the college kids are here," she said.

"Why is that?"

"Well," she said, "there's more going on. You know . . . more action."

After we talked in the lobby for a while, she asked me if I would like to go up to her room. I didn't ask her why and I clearly should have replied "no" or at least "maybe," but I said "sure" and went with her. When I got to her room, the curtains were billowing out from her open beachfront sliding glass doors. The sound of the waves crashing was loud, the lights were very dim, and music was coming from somewhere. She offered me a beer, and I drank it. When she asked, "Would it bother you if I took my bathing suit off?" I didn't answer her.

She then went about her chores in the nude as I sat in a chair watching her. I could see her untanned bikini lines. I had never seen a naked woman casually walking around before, and I tried not to look too surprised. It was a big difference from my Midwestern view of nudity in the shadows. After some time, I said, "I probably should go catch up with my roommate; we were going to have dinner."

"You're welcome to stay here," she said. "There's plenty of room, and I have a big bed."

"That's okay," I said, "I'll just meet up with him since he paid for my trip." She never did put her clothes back on before walking over to unlock the deadbolt and open the door. I left and never saw her again. Four days after my encounter with the naked woman, Chick and I were traveling back to Miami University in his Thunderbird.

In college, I worked more than one job at a time to earn money. As a janitor at the university, I wore a gray coat to identify my position as I emptied ashtrays of cigarette butts, changed light bulbs, and scrubbed the bathrooms. The way people looked at me while I was working stuck in my mind. The work didn't bother me, but wearing the janitor's identifying gray coat did. People still look down on service workers and those in menial jobs based on their uniforms or name tags. We all categorize people by what we see and make assumptions about them.

After that, I worked at a Christmas tree farm outside of town owned by Doc Stephens, my sociology professor. He had short gray hair, a gaunt face, and a large nose from which his voice seemed to be coming. My college friend from grade school, Redhead, who also worked with me at the tree farm, helped set up a paint sprayer filled with green paint. My job was to paint any brown branches a nice shade of pine green.

"If the buyer wants 'em green, then we'll make 'em green," Doc would say.

Today we would be alarmed about the danger of the paint to the consumer.

Redhead and I began selling sweaters and ponchos from our distributor, Zigmund Politi, a Sigma Nu fraternity brother who always seemed have a drink in his hand. He wore a German Army helmet complete with the rectangular side flaps over his ears and, as Dad would say, seemed a little off in the head. Zig told Redhead and me, "Listen, you guys need to go to the Western College for Women," a separate women's school located directly across from Miami's campus. Many at the Western College were from well-to-do eastern, old money families. "You need to tell them the only way they are going to meet any guys from Miami is for them to wear one of your sweaters or ponchos, or even better, both of them." We went there, gave our sales pitch, and it seemed to work because the orders began to arrive.

I met Kathleen King, or Katie, while on a sales visit at Western College. I found out that Katie lived in an exclusive area of Long Island, with her parents, brother, and sister, a place described in a *New York Times* article I read as "a fairy-tale village for those who can afford it." I learned later this area was used as the fictional setting for F. Scott Fitzgerald's *The Great Gatsby*. Katie's dad, a lawyer, was a prominent member of the New York Bar Association. At the time, students were not allowed to have cars at either Miami University or Western College, but Katie had a funny-looking, rectangular-shaped foreign car, a Mercedes-Benz sedan that she drove on weekends and kept hidden in a garage in the poor Black section of town.

Katie was tall, dark haired, beautiful, and probably out of my reach. I still continued to pursue her, even though she refused my invitations to fraternity parties and walks on campus. I tried even harder and kept asking her out. As with my roommate, Chick, it became clear that there was a huge difference in the financial and social positions of various people in the world. It was hard for me to understand then, and it still is.

I told Katie I would like to visit her in New York the next summer during school break. She didn't say no, probably thinking I wouldn't be able to make the trip. I mentioned my plan to Ron Freeman, who was about my age and worked with me that summer on a State of Ohio road crew doing traffic flagging and trash pickup. He suggested we take his old Volkswagen Beetle, leave after work on a Friday afternoon, and drive all night for the seven-hour trip to New York. Ron, who later became a lawyer like his dad, was one of the funniest people I had ever met. Sometimes, during our road crew's lunch break, he would climb up a nearby tree and defy the warnings of our crew boss to come down. I eventually learned that jobs with the State of Ohio, even menial jobs like mine, were based on political patronage. Ron's father was a Republican party leader in the area, so the boss couldn't fire him. I had gotten the summer job when one of our neighbors in Clarksfield Hollow, who worked for the state, suggested to my dad that I go see Ron's father because he could find me work.

Ron and I drove all night without sleeping. Once we got to New York City, we pulled to the curb in the city several times to ask directions, most of which seemed to be intentionally wrong.

Katie's huge two-story home, set back from the street on a large expanse of lawn, was unlike anything I had ever seen. She mentioned her neighbor on one side was a famous singer. Ron drove the red Volkswagen Beetle to the front of the huge circular driveway and blew the horn. Katie came out the front door.

"Wow," she said, "you really did drive all the way here!"

Katie was barefoot and wore summertime clothes, a white cotton blouse with rolled-up sleeves and blue shorts. In contrast, I had on a dark, short-sleeved shirt, dark slacks, and to complete my un-summery look, dark leather shoes. After Ron took a picture of us in front of her home, she invited us in. I think she was surprised but also appreciative of us driving so far just to visit her. She introduced us to her mother and said her father was still at his office. "This is my friend Ben," she said. "He goes to Miami University, next to Western."

Her mother was very pleasant and said, "Katie says you're from Ohio and live on a farm."

Yes," I said, "it's in northern Ohio, near Lake Erie." I added, "I have a sister and three brothers."

"Do they all live in Ohio?" she asked.

"No, just my sister," I said. "My three brothers all live in California."

The home had a lot of bedrooms and a lot of bathrooms, in sharp contrast with our bathless house on Zenobia Road. Katie's mother said, "You must be awfully tired from the long drive."

I said, "Yes, it's quite a drive, especially in Ron's little VW."

"We would love to have you both stay here, and Katie can show you to your rooms."

"That would be great, but we don't want to impose."

"It's no problem," she said. "Why don't you two freshen up, and then we'll have the help fix something to eat." She added, "Katie's father will be coming home late tonight, so you probably won't meet until tomorrow."

The following morning, Ron and I were treated to a large

brunch served on their backyard patio by the family servants. Her dad, Daniel S. King, had given his son and two daughters first names beginning with letters that matched the three letters of his first, middle, and last name. He said, "Katie says you're from Ohio. Is that where you want to live after college?"

"No," I told him, "I'll probably go to California. I have three brothers there."

He said, "Well, I don't know that much about the place, but I do run across attorneys from a school called Stanford. They always think they're a lot smarter than they really are." Ron hadn't said much but did tell Katie's father that his dad was a lawyer in Ohio. "What does he do?" Mr. King asked.

"He's the prosecuting attorney and Republican party chair for our county."

"Does your father enjoy that line of legal work?"

Ron replied, "He says he gets frustrated when trying to submit to the judge some often-used principle and the judge's response is, 'Don't give me any of that constitutional crap.'"

Katie's father chuckled and said, "You must live in the Wild West out there." He proceeded to tell us about his view of life. When someone mentioned that one of their servants had fallen in love, he replied, "She's not capable of love. What does she know?" People can be cruel to others in a way they either don't see or don't care about, something I hadn't experienced while growing up in Brighton.

Katie was not at all standoffish to me during our stay. When Ron and I first arrived, she said, "Let me give you a hug," and then kissed me on the cheek. Traveling all the way to New York that summer, I took a chance that Katie would welcome my visit. She even held my hand under the table at dinner. I felt pleased that Katie and her family accepted me and made me feel welcome. I've learned that people from different backgrounds can still get along and care for each other. We have to push beyond our comfort zone to find that out. Sometimes we can overthink an action we want to take. Taking chances, at least reasonable ones, is what keeps us moving forward.

After leaving Katie's home, we stopped in Greenwich Village to visit her sister at an apartment on Bleeker Street. The Village culture that I saw was yet another learning experience. Those who lived in the Village seemed to be enjoying life and not worrying about jobs or money. Many, I'm sure, including Katie's sister, had money coming from home and didn't need jobs.

Ron and I left after the weekend and drove his Volkswagen back to Ohio and our road crew job. When the summer ended and we returned to college, Katie and I continued to see each other but later drifted apart. When I graduated, she was still attending Western, and I never saw her again. Years later, I received an engraved announcement from her family that she had married.

That fall, I decided to join a fraternity as my brothers Dan and Richard had done before me. My brother Dale, who'd gone to Miami before the rest of us, wasn't the fraternity type, and I soon discovered I felt the same. We had serious fun, but I didn't like the fraternity lifestyle where your life was not your own. It was impossible to have any quiet time as there were always parties, as well as fights around the clock. I thought a lot of the fraternity brothers seemed immature and shallow. This fraternity, originally founded at Virginia Military Institute in the 1800s, was still rooted in prejudice. The song "There Will Never Be a Nigger Sigma Nu" was sung at the fraternity house. We often hear people express opinions about others that are unnecessarily cruel but hesitate to object. We often hear or see things we should confront but choose not to. It's easier to stay silent and not take a stand.

I got a job waiting tables at the house but only lived there one semester. Our cook, Ralph, had two other Black friends who cooked at other fraternities, one called "Daddio" and the other called "Mother Fuck." They often came by the back door of the Sigma Nu kitchen. Ralph helped us find a garage to store the black hearse Dan bought and drove around on weekends and trips back home. Richard had already graduated from Miami by the time I arrived, but he came to visit Dan and me occasionally. Even though Richard and Dan graduated from high school the same year, Dan had worked in construction for two years before starting college and was at Miami both my freshman and sophomore years before graduating.

The hearse was a great conversation piece. We loaded classmates in the back of it for trips to nightspots and to the nearby Indiana border to purchase hard liquor that couldn't be found in the dry town of Oxford. In the days before automobile air-conditioning, the fans installed to keep the casket and flowers cooled made riding around more enjoyable on hot Ohio days.

One Friday night we drove the hearse to the Spatz Show Bar, a nightclub in Hamilton, a small town near Cincinnati. We went to hear the Black performer Bo Diddley, who was becoming popular with his unique sound and square-shaped guitar. We found that except for a few other white college students who came with us, everyone else in the place was Black or "colored," as they were called then. The place was out of control with bottles and glasses flying in all directions, leaving the floor covered in broken glass. We inquired about a hearse parked outside the club; we asked and found out it was Bo Diddley's. He and his band used it to haul their instruments around. Because of the hearse connection, we struck up a conversation with him after the music stopped, asking about his life and music. I heard not very profound words from a well-known person. "Nah, it ain't the music that gives me the thrill, it's the dollar bill," he said. We often mistakenly believe we can find wisdom from someone in a position of authority or fame, and we are especially disappointed when we don't. We spend time searching for answers, only to find that we have the answers and wisdom within ourselves if we would just look.

We convinced Bo Diddley to stop by our fraternity the next day. This turned out to be a wild Saturday afternoon when members of several other fraternities and their dates came by to meet and listen to him.

We drove Dan's hearse home to our farm several times, traveling through small towns, often at fast speeds, and parked it on the farm. Although Mom was shocked by it, she deferred to Dad, who actually enjoyed the humor of it all.

That summer I worked in a factory in Elyria, Ohio. It was hot, noisy, and dirty. I had to join the United Auto Workers Union in order to be an employee there, another new experience for me. The union steward came around and often told us to stop work.

"Hey, college boy!" he yelled. "That box you're lifting may be too heavy. Put it down." This was a new concept to me.

"What do you mean?" I asked.

"Well, sometimes we shut everything down and weigh all the boxes. You see, the boss is always trying to add a pound or two."

This seemed contrary to my work ethic. I thought about the farm, where we were always lifting something that was too heavy and might strain our backs. No one ever said, "Put that down; it might be too heavy." When I got home after working all day at the factory, I could see I had the same dark oily circles around my eyes like my uncle Bob. I also started to see the difference between the more structured life of factory workers, who usually had a repetitive routine with little time or desire for thinking past the factory walls, and farmworkers, who seemed to have more freedom by being outdoors and more interest and curiosity in things around them. This freedom and curiosity about the world around us should be encouraged for all, not just farmers or rural folks.

The years of fraternity parties, school, and summer jobs continued. The next summer, Redhead and I got a job building Interstate 70 in Ohio. When the hiring superintendent asked if we knew how to operate a large multi-wheeled dump truck, Redhead, who had never seen one before in his life, quickly spoke up with confidence, "Sure, we cut our teeth on 'em." We got the job, and after the boss left, we eventually figured out how to get the truck started, shift the gears, and move it forward.

It was on this and my other summer jobs that I came to appreciate the working man's life. On the farm with Dad, we occasionally spoke to each other, but endless work continued mostly without conversation. In the blue-collar workplace, talk among the workers usually involved making fun and harassing others who might take advantage of your job and the feeling that if you didn't, they were going to take advantage of you. Kegley, a big, heavyset guy on the Route 70 job, showed us how to pile the flatbed truck we were directed to load with rocks only on one side. This happened to be the side the boss could see as he drove by at a distance, never getting out of his pickup truck. He also showed us how he put a false bottom in the crew's big five-gallon water cooler to hide ice-cold beer during the hot summer days on the job. The guys on the crew lived and worked for Friday. When they got their paycheck, they drank and gambled a large part of their week's earnings. Although constantly kidding and making fun of each other, there was camaraderie among the workers who enjoyed each other and were willing to help their fellow workers, even me. At eighteen I could drink 3.2 beer and went along to bars with them after work. I liked talking with and listening to them, and I learned about their politics, their women, and their philosophy of life. They had strong and often uncompromising opinions. They talked about how to spot a person who would take advantage of you. So much of what I heard from them was a story of the weak, usually blue-collar workers versus the strong, usually white-collar boss. They were suspicious of authority, whether it was the boss or the government. Questioning authority can be a good trait up to a point. However, when we go too far and question everything, we will be of little use to others or to ourselves.

By my senior year at Miami, I was thinking about going into the foreign service to travel and work in the embassies around the world. My political science college professor suggested I consider law school. I was hesitant about this. I didn't know any lawyers. He said he had gone to law school in San Francisco, at the University of California Hastings College of Law, but he'd ended up in teaching and never practiced law. When my brother Dale learned from Mom that I was unsure about what to do after college, he flew home from California to visit and to help me plan my future. I told Dale I was really interested in the diplomatic corps. He said, "Ben, you don't want to go into the foreign service. You'll never get anywhere in life."

I mentioned my law school professor's suggestion about the Hastings College of Law. "That's what you should do," he said. "Go to law school and become a lawyer. You can come to Fresno and visit while you're in school in San Francisco."

Dale was a true big brother, and I listened to and respected him. I knew he'd had a childhood goal of flying airplanes, and he'd achieved that goal, so I trusted that he knew I could reach my own goal. I took Dale's advice and applied to law school.

Chapter 5

LEAVING OHIO

In the summer of 1963, Mom found an envelope in our mailbox with a San Francisco return address. Our metal mailbox was nailed to the top of a wooden fence post at the end of our driveway. The US Post Office didn't use government vehicles then for rural delivery, and mailmen drove their own cars. Ours drove an old, reddish-brown Oldsmobile. He sat on the passenger's side of his car close to the door so he could access the mailboxes, his legs stretched across the front seat to reach the gas pedal and brake on the driver's side. He always smoked a cigar, and our mail and packages smelled of smoke; to this day, I still correlate the two. When I was young and trying to figure out Santa Claus, the smell of the mailman's cigar smoke signaled the packages came by Oldsmobile and not by sleigh.

The return address on the envelope that Mom brought in read "University of California Hastings College of Law." The letter inside was short and to the point: "You have been admitted as a first-year law student at Hastings College of Law. Classes begin September 5th. You must forward your out-of-state tuition fees."

I knew I had to get organized about leaving Ohio. What would I take with me to a place I had never been? Prior to my acceptance, I hadn't thought much about whether I would get in, or whether I even wanted to go to law school, although Dale had encouraged me, and I respected his advice. "I'm not that familiar with the law school, but I've heard good things about Hastings," he said. I didn't know any lawyers, and Dad knew just one, Harrison Comstock from Wellington. He was respected, and people listened and looked up to him. He seemed friendly and approachable, but at the same time different than salesmen, teachers, or farmers. I thought about his role in the community, and I liked what I saw. I wanted to be like him, and I thought maybe I could.

However, now that it was time to leave for school, I had some doubts. Despite my long-standing interest in adventure and travel, suddenly I wasn't so sure about leaving Ohio. I felt secure on the farm where I had spent my life until then, and I had only been out of Ohio three or four times, and never west of Illinois. I'd enjoyed my time in Ohio, especially that particular summer working for Tony Springer's family business.

Tony had graduated a year ahead of me at Wellington High School. His family owned a number of retirement homes where they cared for aging patients with a variety of ailments. The summer before leaving for law school, I helped build a new facility next to an existing one they owned in Amherst, Ohio. It was hard, hot work, but Tony kept everyone laughing with his jokes and antics. An occupant of the rest home came up to our job site one afternoon and stood looking down at me in the trench I was digging. Tony introduced the old guy to me, who smiled and showed off the few teeth he had left, yellow and stained with tobacco juice and nicotine.

"Son," he said to me, "when I was your age, I had a construction crew of forty horses and a hundred men." He stopped and collected his thoughts. "No," he said, "I'm pretty sure it was forty men and a hundred horses."

Tony jumped into the conversation, to save the old guy from further embarrassment.

"It was a helluva lotta men and horses, right, Claude?"

"Yeah," he replied.

Tony's family owned a summer cabin on Lake Erie about twenty miles from our farm. The place sat back some from the water in an area of big trees that gave so much shade it felt cool even in the midday Ohio summer heat.

Usually consumed by constant work on the farm, I couldn't see vacations as useful or productive, but Lake Erie was different and fascinated me. On our farm, we could see only fields and trees in all directions. On the shore of Lake Erie, I noticed a lot of people riding around in boats not working or doing much of anything. The lake's sounds of seagulls, foghorns, and boat engines sounds made me think of far-off, adventurous places. Lake Erie had a pungent odor of fish and oil and boat exhaust. The south shore of the lake, while only about twenty miles from our farm, felt to me like a distant foreign country. On the farm, folks might go to a drive-in movie, or to the Dairy Queen for dessert, but almost every day was filled with work. Farmers didn't take vacations in the summertime, which Dad pretty well summed up when he said, "You have to make hay while the sun shines." I understood and came to appreciate his approach to life. Get things done; don't waste time or talk about what you intend to do.

Except for the year I worked for Tony's family, I spent summers on road construction or home building crews, and at night, always helped Dad with the farmwork. I liked the construction jobs and being around the workers who always referred to me as "the college boy." They usually spoke of what their "old lady" had packed in their lunch pail and the beers they would have on Friday after work. I began forming my later opinion of the difference between white-collar and blue-collar workers and tended to feel more in common with the latter. After I got home from the road construction job, Dad and I often worked late into the night, stacking hay in the barn that he had baled earlier in the day. On the days I was with the construction crew, either Mom or a hired hand drove the tractor for Dad, who loaded the bales on the hay wagon. If I got home in time, we still did some baling before the evening dampness settled over the rows of raked, sweet-smelling alfalfa.

Baling hay, stacking the bales on the wagon, and putting it away high in the mow was hard, hot, dusty work. Occasionally the farmwork became more efficient and, consequently, a little easier. This was the case when Dad bought a New Holland hay baler to tie the hay bales automatically with twine. Before Dad got the new machine, we used an old wire tie model that required one person to drive the tractor, one person to drop the bale divider board in the slot at just the right time, and one person to poke the wires through the hay and hand tie the wires to hold the bale together, in addition to someone on the wagon to load the bales. If the divider board was dropped too early, it would split the board and plug the machine, and if too late, the hay bale would be torn apart and have to be pulled out of the baler by hand and fed back through the machine. While I appreciated the lesser amount of work because of the baler, although I didn't say it, I missed working together with my three brothers on the old machine, even under the extremely hot, tough conditions of Ohio summers.

The work of putting up hay was hard, hot, and dirty, and only after dark would the temperature finally begin to cool. The summer air was heavy and sultry with high humidity. The small alfalfa leaves and the even smaller timothy hay seeds stuck to the hair on your head and arms and mixed with sweat that ran down your neck and back. The old-timers working on farms in the summer wore long underwear covering their arms and legs, which seemed contrary to common sense. However, I found the long under-wear became wringing wet with sweat, and the air, or better yet, a breeze, cooled the wearer as the sweat evaporated.

Despite the hard work and tough conditions, I didn't complain that much except sometimes to fit in with the others. The main difference between me and the rest of the crew was the satisfaction and accomplishment I felt in the often hard physical labor I did on the farm and construction jobs.

In later years, even though I still felt comfortable, secure, and pleased with where I was in my life, I wanted to do something more, to move on and to push myself to work harder. I've wondered if others felt this way as well but never figured out how to bring it up in conversation. We need to set our own course, even when we encounter comments or criticism from others who may have their own shortcomings. And if working hard is part of the route we take, we don't need validation from anyone else.

One late summer afternoon shortly after I'd been accepted to Hastings, I stood in our soybean field beside the big red cow barn and looked west. I tried to imagine the endless miles of highways ahead to California, where I had never been.

I stood on our land and thought about the days growing up there and our neighbors. About two hundred yards to the west from where I stood that day, a fence row thick with weeds and bushes was the only thing that separated our farm from Charlie Leider's place. When he was in college, my brother Dale would land his small, single-engine Stinson airplane in this field that we always planted to soybeans. Dale's membership in the college flying club at Miami University gave him access to an airplane that he would fly home to the farm on occasion. I can still see him up in the sky circling the farm before landing next to our house. As his little brother, I looked up to and admired Dale. Seeing him fly overhead and doing what he loved to do made me very proud. In order to surprise our nearby neighbors, Dan, Richard, and I went out to the field to greet Dale as the plane rolled to a stop. Dan asked Dale if we could move the plane over to the front yard. Dale replied, "It's okay with me—just don't mess up anything." Before we moved the plane, we asked Dale to take a picture of us. We then pushed the plane out of the field and down Zenobia Road to our house. In the picture Dale took that day of Dan, Richard, and me in front of the plane in the soybean field, I stood between my brothers with my back to the camera, displaying my jokester traits.

Beyond the field and beyond my sight, I knew Francis Nestor's place was at the intersection of Butler and Zenobia Roads. Farther to the west on Zenobia Road, I thought of Clarksfield Hollow and Norwalk, the Huron County seat, and finally Fremont, the birthplace and home of President Rutherford B. Hayes and the town used as the setting of Sherwood Anderson's *Winesburg, Ohio,* a book that opened many eyes and minds to the inner lives of those who lived down the street. We think we know them, but often we really don't.

I knew that even farther west would be the Ohio border, Indiana, Illinois, and then Iowa, Nebraska, and the western states of Wyoming, Utah, Nevada, and after all of that would be California, where my three brothers now lived. This was my greatest opportunity to satisfy my urge for adventure, and so, between the security of home and the unknown, I chose the latter.

Once I'd decided to go to California, I faced the problem of getting there. I didn't have a car and had been driving Dad's truck or Mom's Pontiac that summer.

While in Wellington one afternoon that summer, I ran into Dr. John Ripkin, a DO, or doctor of osteopathic medicine, from the

Cleveland area who came to town to hold office hours every week. Ripkin had a new and unusual car called an Avanti, something I hadn't seen before. I learned later the car was only manufactured for about nine years, and there were none in our area.

Ripkin suggested to me, "Why don't you drive my car to San Francisco? I'm flying out there in September for a lengthy stay. We can meet up, and then I'll have a car to drive while I'm in California."

I thought this was a great idea and said so to Mom.

"Absolutely not!" Mom said without even hesitating. I couldn't understand her resistance to the idea at the time. This was one of Mom's traits: make a quick decision, stick with it, and don't waste time explaining things. I wouldn't learn her reason until later.

Dad could see I wasn't getting anywhere with the Dr. Ripkin idea and suggested I look in the newspaper ads for rides to California. On weekdays the *Elyria Chronicle-Telegram* was delivered at our house, and on Sunday the *Cleveland Plain Dealer*. Flying wasn't common at the time, especially for a farm boy just out of college. I had never ridden a train and couldn't imagine taking one that far, so I didn't even consider it. Dad thought people might advertise for rides by automobile. Sure enough, I found an ad in the Sunday *Cleveland Plain Dealer* placed by a man looking for riders to help him drive and share the gas expense from Ohio back to California. *WANTED: RIDERS TO CALIFORNIA. 216 647-3323.* I called the number in the ad. The man who answered was abrupt and to the point.

"Look, I'm here in Cleveland to see my kids. They're with the ex-wife. I need to get outta here and back to California. Can ya drive a car?"

"Yeah, sure, I know how to drive," I replied.

"Well, it's gonna cost you, and you're gonna have to take turns driving cause we ain't gonna stop."

He continued to jabber, blurting out, "Do ya know where the turnpike is?"

"Yeah, of course I know where it is," I said, wanting to seem as worldly as I could.

Then he said, "Meet me August fifteenth at ten in the morning at the Elyria-Lorain turnpike interchange. And don't bring much cause I ain't got any room."

"Okay, I'll be there," I said, thinking to myself that he sounded like a jerk and very bossy on the telephone.

He added, "Don't be late or I'll leave ya."

I only had a couple of weeks left until the day to meet my travel partner. I finished up my summer construction job and spent the rest of my time helping Dad with as much farmwork as we could get done. As the time to leave home came nearer, I began to notice things more acutely. The sweet smell of fresh-mowed clover with its rose-colored flowers and the earthy smell of alfalfa filled the summertime air on the farm. A very hot, humid summer day in August would soon be followed by heavy, black, rain-soaked clouds out of the west. These summer thunderstorms could be fierce. Beginning with the proverbial calm before the storm, the breeze stopped, the air became still, and the leaves began to curl. The humidity thickened, and the air became heavy and sticky. Large, black, ominous-looking clouds appeared on the western horizon as the wind picked up and became stronger. Dad said the thickness of the gray clouds around the black rain clouds determined the amount of wind in the storm. "Look at the leaves," he would say. "They're starting to curl up. Rain's coming."

One of the worst storms rolled across our farm just before I left for California. Out from the west, long bolts of lightning shot toward the farm, and then came sharp cracks of thunder as the storm approached. I could see and hear it in the distance, as the air smelled fresh and cool from the distant rain moving closer and dropping the temperature. The sky turned black and gray with streaks of yellow, and as Dad said, the wind seemed to be coming from the gray clouds and was getting stronger by the minute. The wind blew a shed off its foundation on the Foster place across Zenobia Road. Lightning struck the small barn there, and the fire that followed burned it to the ground. The wind began to howl, the bright midafternoon August sunshine disappeared, and it grew very dark. It was too late for Dad and me to run from the fields to the house or barn. Dad said, "Just lie flat and keep your head down as much as you can. Don't worry, son, we'll be okay." I think my uneven voice gave my fright away, and, as with so many times in my life, Dad was a calming force.

The rain came down hard, big drops that felt like stones hitting my neck and back. The big drops, according to Dad, meant the storm would pass quickly. The wind howled, and loose boards and tin ripped from the shed roof and shot across the open fields. Branches broke from the trees in the lane near the woods and blew across the fields in front of us. Then the storm ended as quickly as it had begun. The bright, searing hot sun reappeared within fifteen or twenty minutes. Dad and I got up off the ground, soaked to the skin. Dad headed for the house to dry off, but I lingered for a while, wondering if California had the same kind of weather.

I started to organize what I would take to California, and it wasn't much, just some jeans and long-sleeved shirts for winter and my college summer clothes, madras plaid shirts and khaki pants. I didn't know much about San Francisco, but I was pretty sure it wasn't going to snow, so I didn't take the big parka I'd worn at Miami University in the winter. Along with my clothes, I packed my favorite family picture of Mom and Dad (taken next to our farm pond) with our dog, King, a big German shepherd mix. I wanted to fit everything in one suitcase, but I thought I might be able to get Jack, my ride to California, to let me take a cardboard box as well.

Jack had warned me in our short phone call not to bring much. Dad got out the dark brown, hard-plastic Samsonite suitcase he and Mom had used when they drove to Arkansas to visit Betty. It wouldn't hold all my stuff, so Dad found a stiff cardboard box with fold-over flaps at Irish's Market in Wellington that he said should work fine.

I stuffed my clothes into the Samsonite suitcase and managed to fit the rest of my belongings into Dad's cardboard box. We talked about the money I would need, and Dad gave me five twenty-dollar bills and a checkbook from the First Wellington Bank, where I had deposited my summer construction job earnings and the first installment of the loan from the Production Credit Association in Norwalk. The business of the association was to loan money to farmers to finance crop production, which they paid back when the crop was harvested. With me present, Dad explained to the association manager that I wanted to go to law school in California and needed money. They thought it an unusual request but seemed impressed with a farm boy trying to better himself and gave me the loan under Dad's signature. I drew on the loan during my three years in law school and paid it back over an eight-year period after I graduated.

Dad tied the cardboard box with bright yellow binder twine and did two loops around the hard-plastic Samsonite suitcase just in case it popped open. We used a lot of this type of twine on the farm to tie bags of grain and bales of hay. The color came from some chemical treatment that stopped rats from gnawing through the twine. That day, it kept all my stuff from spilling out. When it was time to leave the house to meet my ride out West, Mom said, "Honey, you need to be very careful," as we stood in the kitchen. "I

miss you already." She kissed my right cheek. Walking me toward
the door, she said, "I know you're on edge, but you can do this."
Mom could be as endearing as she was insensitive to anyone she
thought was a loudmouth or a show-off. This day, she was at her
finest and most loving.

As she walked me out to the driveway where Dad was waiting
for me with the car running, Dad said, "Son, you look concerned."

"I am, Dad," I replied. "This is something I really want to do,
but I'm kind of nervous."

"You'll be fine," he said.

Dad and I left our farm on Zenobia Road in the two-tone
brown family Pontiac and drove toward the Elyria-Lorain turnpike interchange where I had agreed to meet my ride. We passed
Brighton, where I'd gone to grade school, and the little town of
Pittsfield that had been devastated years before by an Easter Sunday tornado. We drove past Oberlin, where I'd first eaten pizza
and seen large numbers of Black people. We headed toward Lake
Erie, where I'd partied at Tony Springer's place. The farther from
home we drove, the more anxious I started to feel about what I
was doing and all I was leaving behind. I started talking faster,
asking questions of Dad about his taking care of the farm in my
absence. Dad replied, "I'll be okay. Remember, you've been away at
school for a few years anyway."

Dad and I waited alongside the highway at the rest stop that
afternoon for what seemed like a very long time. We didn't say much
to each other. When you grow up on a farm and you're with your
Dad every day from sunup to sundown, you don't need to talk much.

About an hour after the time he said he would arrive, my ride
finally showed up. He skidded to a stop on the shoulder of the
turnpike, sending gravel flying in all directions.

He jumped out of the car and started shaking my hand,
pumping his arm up and down. "You must be Ben. I'm Jack, nice

to meet you." After he stopped talking, I was finally able to introduce him to Dad. As I came to appreciate more and more over the years, Dad could size up someone in about thirty seconds and was usually right. I caught Dad giving this guy his standard once-over, but this time, I knew I had to ignore his negative impression, because I'd already made my decision to leave.

Jack had another rider with him too. "Hi, I'm Bruce," he said, as he shook hands with Dad and me. "Guess I answered the same newspaper ad you did. I'm from Cleveland." He then explained that he was the nephew of the mayor of Cleveland.

"Really," I said. I was more concerned about going on a long trip with people I had never met, to a place I had never been, in a car I had never ridden in.

Dad helped me load the cardboard box and Samsonite suitcase into Jack's car. At the time, farm boys usually didn't kiss their Dad or say, "I love you," and so we just hugged, and then he turned away. I couldn't see his tears until he turned back to say, "Goodbye, son; be careful." We drove off, leaving Dad still standing alongside the highway.

We left the rest area heading west on the turnpike toward the Ohio-Indiana border and then on to Illinois and beyond. Indiana was flat and without any distinguishing landmarks that I could see. I had only been about a mile inside the southern Indiana border across from Miami University to buy hard liquor, which wasn't sold in the dry county on the Ohio side.

As the miles wore on, I wasn't prepared for what I saw. As every first-time cross-country traveler knows, the scenery changes dramatically the farther west you go. Western Ohio, Indiana, Illinois, and parts of Iowa looked much like our farm, with tall stalks of green corn and fields of soybeans. Then the land flattened out. The August sky seemed bigger and bluer. Mountains began to appear in the distance.

Before the big interstate highways were built, the only way across the country was Highway 40 in the north or Route 66 in the south. These were still mostly two-lane roads with lots of local traffic and small towns to drive through. After driving for only a few hours, Jack and Bruce began to argue. Bruce took the first turn relieving Jack at driving, but Jack didn't like the way Bruce drove and started complaining.

Jack asked bluntly, "Are you queer or what?" Bruce didn't answer. After that episode, Bruce was relegated by Jack to the back seat for the remainder of the trip. He never drove the car or sat in the front seat again.

Jack had an opinion on everything and everybody—always talking, loud to the point of yelling, and waving his arms around. He wore a shirt with a collar, front, and short sleeves, but no back. He tried to explain. "It's really hot out there," he said, pointing west where we were headed. "I ain't got air-conditioning." He was trying to convince me it was a practical way to keep cool.

He continued to shout out advice as the miles wore on.

"Never blow the horn when you're next to the passenger side of another car," he said.

"Why?" I asked.

"Cause, the other guy'll pull over and cause a wreck."

"Okay, sure," I said, thinking through all of his talk that he knew much less than he claimed to.

After the Ohio, Indiana, and Illinois Turnpikes, we continued our journey west to Iowa and then Nebraska. The air smelled sweet through our open windows, and I could tell it was coming from the rose-colored buds on the alfalfa plants in the nearby fields. The sight and smell of those fields reminded me of Ohio. In Cheyenne, Wyoming, I first felt the difference between Ohio and the West. We stopped at a gas station with an attached small coffee shop. The men at the counter wore straight-legged jeans, unlike what we wore on the farm, with cowboy boots and long-sleeved shirts with metal buttons. They didn't look anything like the bib overall–wearing farmers I was used to seeing. They seemed like cowboys. There were few towns and fewer people as we headed toward Utah. Now the landforms changed even more with tall mountains and golden fields leading to the tall peaks. I could clearly see what I thought must be the Rocky Mountains in the distance.

Our days and nights were the same. We never slept in a bed and never stopped the car except to fill up with gas. When we did stop at a gas station, we took turns with one using the restroom, if there was one, while the other filled the gas tank. By the second day of driving, the sandwiches Mom had made for me and the apples I'd brought along had all been eaten, and after that we lived on snacks from the gas stations. We'd leave the station with enough junk food to hold us over until we needed another tank of gas. Jack and I each took turns sleeping in the front passenger seat as the other one drove. Bruce remained in the back seat with no chance of redemption.

After about fifty hours of round-the-clock, nonstop driving, we crossed the border of Nevada into California late one night. I took a deep breath and imagined what must be outside in the dark. I didn't realize that I would have seen brown mountains and dead grass, not the Midwestern greenness of the summer. The car was struggling and making noises as we drove in the steeper mountains, and I wondered if we were nearing the ocean. As Midwestern folks, we seemed to think anywhere in California was near the ocean.

Jack told us, "Look, this is where the Donner Party crossed. They ate each other to stay alive. Did you know that?"

I didn't even answer him. For almost three thousand miles, I had listened to his small amount of knowledge on every big subject in the world. I couldn't see anything out of the car windows at all. It was pitch-black dark. Sure, I knew the story of the Donner Party, but I'd learned from Dad growing up on the farm to "never flaunt your own intelligence around someone with very little of their own."

I didn't realize that Sacramento wasn't just next door to Oakland where I needed to be. When Jack let me out at the Sacramento Greyhound Bus Station on L and Ninth Streets, it was about one o'clock in the morning. I unloaded my cardboard box and the Samsonite suitcase in front of the station.

"See ya, good luck!" Jack yelled as he drove off, never looking back. Bruce, the other passenger, got out and went his own way into Sacramento. I never saw or heard from either of them again.

A metal bulletin board on the bus station wall had a long list of schedules. After looking it over, I had two choices: wait until the next day for the express bus or take a local that night to Oakland. I didn't know anything about Greyhound buses and had never heard of the term "local" bus. I decided not to wait and bought a ticket for the local. I loaded the cardboard box and suitcase on and off several buses that night as I learned the designation "local" meant stopping at nearly every town along the route.

I began to see that bus stations all look and smell the same. They are home to the fringes of society, people passing through to get out of the summer heat or winter cold, out of a bad marriage or relationship and into a new one. The stations are full of cigarette smoke, down-and-out travelers, and sad goodbyes. The ticket seller is usually a lady with a lot of years showing on her face, bad teeth, and worn and wrinkled skin from too many years of nicotine and late nights. The one in Sacramento that night was seated behind a plastic see-through window with a hole at the bottom to talk through and exchange tickets and money.

The next morning, I finally got to Oakland. Days had gone by since I'd slept in a bed or taken a shower. However, having grown up on our farm without a bathroom or shower, it didn't matter that much to me. I unloaded the box and my suitcase from the bus one last time and moved to a new form of transportation. The taxi dropped me off at my brother Richard's Oakland apartment. His apartment lease had a month remaining, and before I left Ohio, he'd called to suggest I stay there until I found a place of my own. Richard had already left for New York, and his apartment was mostly empty. I got the key he'd left for me from the apartment manager and let myself in. Overcome with exhaustion, I fell asleep on the couch, leaving worry about the rest of my journey and the rest of my life for another time.

The next morning, I looked out Richard's apartment window and saw only concrete sidewalks and more apartments. The streets were starting to fill with cars and people. I needed to get to San Francisco, as I was running out of time to check into Hastings Law School. After checking around, I found that without a car, I needed to take a city transit bus. It was early morning as the bus groaned and clanked across the Bay Bridge deck. I could see the San Francisco skyline out the window. The sun glared off the tall buildings to the water below. The city's buildings were so close to each other and contrasted with the beautiful setting surrounding them. The bus left the elevated bridge at the Fremont Street exit and then down to the city below.

The bus wound up at the Mission Street terminal in San Francisco, along with dozens of other noisy, black-smoke-belching city buses. From there I got a transfer ticket and took another new form of transportation, a streetcar that took me to my law school at the intersection of McAllister and Hyde Streets in the Civic Center area of downtown San Francisco.

The school was not what I had expected. There was no tree-lined campus like the college I'd just left. The law school building itself was situated next to the Federal Courthouse, the California

State Office Building, and San Francisco's City Hall. This would be the first of many shocks to my Ohio farm background that I would encounter in the coming years. There was only one stark law school building. Inside the building, I found the "New Student" registration window and got in line. There, while waiting, I struck up a conversation with the guy next to me.

"Hi, I'm Ben Ewell from Ohio," I said, introducing myself. He was James L. Condren, who liked to be called "Duke," a fellow first-year law student from upstate New York.

"I need to find a place to live," he said. "Do you know what you plan to do?"

I said, "I need to find a place too. Maybe we could room together."

"Good idea," he replied. This brief encounter began a friendship that lasted my entire time in San Francisco. Duke, like Dad, never seemed to be worried about things you couldn't do anything about. "Don't worry," he would say. "It'll work out."

Chapter 6

HAIGHT-
ASHBURY

Jumping off the 71 Muni Bus that August day in 1963 at the San Francisco intersection of Haight and Ashbury Streets started a new life for me.

The beefy bus driver yelled, "Hey, kid, ain't ya ever been on a bus before?" He could see I was trying to push down the steel plate in the bottom step to open the rear doors. He was right; I hadn't been on this kind of a bus before. When the doors jerked open with a loud bang, I grabbed my cardboard box and brown plastic Samsonite suitcase and jumped to the street. The doors slammed shut behind me as the bus roared westerly down Haight Street toward Golden Gate Park, and I looked around for 72 Central Avenue.

As soon as Duke and I agreed to become roommates, I had started looking in the rentals section of the newspaper for a place to stay. I found a furnished room listed in an area of San Francisco I had not heard of, called Haight-Ashbury. The advertised rent of seventy-five dollars a month fit our combined budget, so I called the number in the ad. The guy who answered the phone said if I wanted the place, I had better hurry. I told Duke I'd ride the bus that afternoon to take a look.

72 Central Avenue was a run-down, faded brown, two-story Victorian-style rooming house at the intersection of Central Avenue and Haight Street, one block east of the soon-to-be-famous Haight-Ashbury intersection. I walked up the steps to the front door and rang the buzzer. A short, fat, balding man opened the door and showed me the room for rent, with its two small single beds, a cabinet, a curved window facing Central Avenue, and no bathroom or closet. It was just inside the front door with an entry on the right. It seemed to be the former living room of the house. One small, closet-sized bathroom down the hall would serve the needs of the grumpy manager, Duke, and me.

I gave it little thought, in my typical decision-making style, and said, "I'll take it, and there's gonna be two of us. I brought my stuff with me."

"Yeah, okay," the manager replied. "Just pay on time and don't stay in the bathroom all day. When I gotta go, I ain't gonna wait for you or nobody."

When I got back to downtown San Francisco, Duke was waiting for me.

"I looked at the room today," I said.

"Well, what do you think?"

"I think it will be okay," I said. "I left my stuff there."

Duke said, "Jump on the back of my bike." With me on the back, Duke and I rode out to Central Avenue that afternoon on his motorcycle.

"Not bad," Duke said as we walked up the steps and went inside. "There's not much to it, but then we don't need much." Duke said he would get his stuff and be back later that night. With that, we paid the landlord seventy-five dollars for the first month's rent.

About three months after moving into the Central Avenue rooming house, I watched Jack Ruby shoot Lee Harvey Oswald on live television. Before that, Walter Cronkite on November 22 had described the First Lady's bloodstained pink dress, which appeared colorless on our little black-and-white screen. In this era before TV reality shows and social media, we were not prepared to see tragedy unfolding on live television. In the midst of this national crisis it struck me that even in a time of tragedy, Jacqueline Kennedy seemed so calm and beautiful when she accompanied her husband's coffin on the return trip to Washington, DC, aboard Air Force One. I could not have known then that, years later, I would try to present the same calm appearance to others as I learned of the murder of my brother Dale by a gunshot to the back of the head.

Seventy-Two Central Avenue backed up to Buena Vista Park, a small, green oasis in an otherwise congested urban setting.

I discovered that Haight-Ashbury consisted of about nine city blocks, and around 250 acres, almost the same size as our Ohio farm and the Foster place combined. It took its name from the intersection of two streets: Haight Street, probably named after pioneer San Franciscan Henry Haight, and Ashbury Street, apparently named after Munroe Ashbury, a member of the 1870 San Francisco Board of Supervisors. The neighborhood was bordered by Golden Gate Park on the west, Panhandle Park on the north, Buena Vista Park on the east, and Ashbury Heights on the south. Cool, quiet Pacific Ocean fog rolled across Haight-Ashbury almost every afternoon.

The written history of the area indicated that by the 1950s, San Francisco residents had begun moving out of the city, and the area declined. Former single-family grand Victorian homes, complete with colorful exterior gingerbread trim, became rooming houses divided into multiple cheap living spaces like the one we rented. In the 1960s, the area's cheap rooming house rent became a lure for college students from the nearby University of

San Francisco and the San Francisco State campus on Nineteenth Avenue, just as it did for me as a law school student.

Because I didn't have a car, I rode the city bus back and forth to law school every day. Duke and I had different class schedules; my classes were in the morning and his in the afternoon. Duke would ride his motorcycle to Hastings from our Haight-Ashbury rooming house for his afternoon classes, while I rode the bus to the morning sessions. Duke also worked part-time at night as an underground garage attendant. We got along with each other. I stayed late after class some nights to study in the San Francisco City Law Library located on the top floor of the majestic, gold-domed City Hall, just down McAllister Street from Hastings Law School.

Melvin Belli, the white-haired, bombastic, larger-than-life San Francisco lawyer occasionally came to the law library at night to do research when I was there. Driving a Silver Cloud Rolls-Royce, he would park in the spot in front of City Hall clearly marked, "Reserved: Mayor of San Francisco." The young, African American City Hall night attendant with whom I became acquainted told me how Belli would park in the mayor's spot, step out of his Rolls-Royce, climb up the several levels of steps of the City Hall's grand entrance, and almost always say, "Boy, that's Mr. Belli's car. Don't let anyone touch it."

The young attendant's automatic response would be, "Yes, sir. Yes, sir, Mr. Belli."

Belli, known as the King of Torts, had been to Hastings a couple of times to lecture our torts class, invited by his friend and our professor, William Prosser. Belli gave hilarious animated lectures in Prosser's class, walking back and forth across the front of the lecture hall, gesturing with his arms. He appeared perfectly groomed with long, silver hair, a dark double-breasted pin-striped suit, and a folded handkerchief in his upper left breast pocket. A story circulated that the American Bar Association had become concerned about Belli's outspoken manner and threatened to remove him from membership. Belli laughed off the Bar Association's proposed action, reportedly commenting to the press something to the effect that, "expulsion from the American Bar Association would be like throwing me out of the Book of the Month Club." We can probably learn from Belli's actions. He was well-known, successful, and flamboyant, but he had the ability to go against the establishment in a way that was entertaining and not mean-spirited. Sometimes, we can best make a point or take a stand by using just enough humor to lessen the impact of our objection.

When I first arrived in Haight-Ashbury, it was like living in a small community, similar to rural towns near our Ohio farm. There was a small Chinese-operated market across from our rooming house, and down the street were a laundry, a barber shop, and a restaurant. Duke and I shopped for groceries at the Safeway farther down Haight Street. Duke liked corned beef, cabbage, onions, and other items I couldn't really stand, but we managed to find a balance in our food preferences and eating habits.

As we went about our errands, people were friendly, outgoing, and greeted one another on the street with a "Hey, how's it going?" like they had in the places where Duke and I had grown up. But in the coming months, the area's atmosphere began to change from a small-town feel to urban chaos. With that change, stores on Haight Street began installing iron bars or shutters on doors and windows and closing up at night. During this time Haight Street, once busy with cars and local pedestrians, became harder to drive on because of all the people in the street. Before too long the street was closed to cars and open only to foot traffic. The constant sound of loud music could be heard blaring around the clock from the bars, streets, and apartments.

In the 1960s, street musicians played everywhere. Bands and musical groups, many of which later became well-known, began forming in Haight-Ashbury, and the Fillmore Auditorium featured many rock groups of the era. The first time I went to the Fillmore, motivated more by curiosity than music, I suffered culture shock. The ear-splitting noise, strobe lights, heavy smoke, drug sales, presence of marijuana, and wall-to-wall crowds jangled me. It was nearly impossible to see or hear the bands, and clearly no one cared. Perhaps it was my rural Ohio roots or my focus on succeeding in law school that caused my lack of interest in exploring this new culture a great deal.

While drugs, the hippie culture, and music groups surrounded me, I was more of an observer than a participant. Living in Haight-Ashbury, I could see what was going on, but I walked around those drunk, overdosed, and sleeping on the sidewalks. Although my Midwest background led me generally to be helpful to others, I tried to ignore the hippies, the homeless, and the drug dealers. I never completely sorted out in my mind my contradictory views between alcohol, which I consumed at the time in substantial quantities, and drugs, which I did not. While I drank and got drunk, drugs just didn't interest me. Duke drank a lot of alcohol but always said, "I think it's my Irish coming out." The drugs in the neighborhood didn't interest him either.

After class one day, I found a note on the law school bulletin board that said I should call Dr. Ripkin, a "friend from Ohio" at the St. Francis Hotel in Union Square. Ripkin was from Cleveland but came to Wellington two or three days a week to hold office hours. I called the hotel, and he said he had just arrived from Ohio and would like to get together. He invited me to meet him at the Oak Bar at the St. Francis.

"Well, I see you found another way to California," he said.

After I shook his hand, I said, "Yeah, I got a ride with a kind of crazy guy, but we made it."

"How's law school?"

"A lot different from Ohio," I said. We sat at the bar and talked about Ohio and his visits to Wellington. After a couple of beers, he suggested we go to his room to get away from the noise in the bar so we could continue to talk. We were both silent as we rode the elevator to his floor. Shortly after we entered his room, he said, "Why don't you take off your coat." I did take off my coat and laid it over a chair, which I sat in while we continued to talk.

Later he suggested that I should stay with him since it was getting late. "This is a pretty good-sized bed, but if you don't want to sleep in the same bed, I can just fall asleep in the chair."

I said, "I think I should go. I'll just catch a cab." I grabbed my coat and moved toward the door.

"No, just stay here. I want you to stay," he insisted as he moved his pudgy frame in front of the door to block me. We pushed back and forth, but I was able to grab the door handle, release the chain lock, push him aside, and leave. There were no goodbyes.

I thought back to my plan to drive his new Avanti from Ohio to San Francisco and how Mom had said, "Absolutely not!" I never saw or spoke to him again and didn't mention it to Mom. When Duke got home from work that night, I told him. "Sounds to me like a full-service doctor," Duke said with a chuckle.

As soon as I awoke the next morning, I went for a walk. I thought it would block out the stress of the strange incident from the night before with Dr. Ripkin. There were lots of people on the sidewalk that morning, and I took some time as I walked down Haight Street to think about my neighbors. Most were hippies, usually white, middle-class kids and young adults who I'm sure were not nearly as poor as they wanted to appear. There were Black people, but not that many, and the same with Latinos. I'd had limited interaction with both groups in Ohio, and that mostly continued here.

Hells Angels members were around, as their San Francisco headquarters was nearby at Ashbury and Waller. The area as well as the city itself was home to lots of Asians, particularly Chinese. The owners of the little corner market and the laundry were both Asian. They seemed quiet, always busy minding their own business. Years before, they had worked and died to build the railroad west and other things deemed as progress at the time. We often think of the world or actions as divided between us and them, "them" being those who look, sound, or act differently from us. The more we can move away from this division, the better we can understand and appreciate our differences.

I learned later from a book about the Haight that my neighbors at 710 Ashbury, just a block from our rooming house, were Jerry Garcia and his bandmates. The gatherings there promoted many other neighborhood singers, musicians, and writers. If I passed these artists and musicians on the street, I didn't recognize them.

In 1963, the same year I moved into Haight-Ashbury, twenty-year-old Janis Joplin, from the oil-drilling town of Port Arthur, Texas, moved to San Francisco and, according to records from that time, landed first at 635 Ashbury Street and later at 122 Lyon Street, one block north of Haight Street. A poster of Janis still hangs prominently on the entrance wall of the Fillmore along with Jimi Hendrix, who lived at 1524A Haight Street. The posters of the day depicted Janis in her wild-colored poncho dress; she became one of the symbols of Haight-Ashbury music in the 1960s and afterward. I thought about how the hippies tried so hard to be different from the rest of society and ended up wanting others to conform to their way of seeing the world. We see this often in life where, on the surface, someone tries to take on a different role, but it's only superficial. Eventually the real person will emerge.

After several months, Duke and I moved a half block south up the hill to the corner of Central Avenue and Waller Street. The Waller Street apartment location with its two-story, tan stucco walls, contrasted sharply with the Victorian homes on either side of 72 Central Avenue. We lived on the second floor of this new location, which appeared to have recently been built or remodeled.

One weekend I rode the Greyhound bus to Fresno to visit my brothers Dan and Dale. Dale, with Dan in his car, picked me up at the Fresno bus station. Dale said, "I'm going out to my ranch. Do you guys want to ride along?"

"Sure," I said, "I'd like to go."

"I'll show you the new trees Glee and I planted." Dale's orange groves were east of Fresno where he worked almost every weekend doing a lot the ranch work himself along with my sister-in-law, Glee. On the way to the ranch, Dale asked me lots of questions about law school. "How do you like it so far?"

"I like it, but boy, it's different from Brighton," I replied.

"I'll bet it is," Dale said.

I thought how well he would know, having gone from Brighton to living in Texas, Arizona, and Los Angeles after his time in the Air Force.

Dale said, "If I can ever help you, just let me know. After all, I kinda got you into this."

When we arrived at Dale's ranch, there was a big red tractor parked by his shed with one back wheel missing. "Why don't you guys take a picture of me?" he said. "I've got a camera in the car." He bent down out of sight of the jack under the tractor, making it appear that he himself was holding it up.

After returning from Dale's ranch, I told Dan that I needed to find something to drive. "I saw a car for sale," he said. "It might be just what you need." I bought the car for $250. The small English Ford was parked along Fresno's Blackstone Avenue with a "FOR SALE" sign in the window along with a warning in huge letters that read, "AS IS." Today, a buyer might have some rights after the purchase of a damaged car, but this was the era, as described in our torts class, of "caveat emptor."

The car's front-end grille had been smashed in, and I found that one of the four gears did not work as I drove it back to San Francisco. When it rained, the car leaked, and water collected in the back-seat footwells, requiring any passengers riding with me to lift their feet to the back seat to keep from getting them wet. When the car wouldn't start on its own, I would shift to first gear, push in the clutch, and let it roll down the garage ramp toward Waller Street below, letting out the clutch at just the right time while shouting out the window to warn people to get out of the way as the car shot into the street.

Law school, at least Hastings, was not like the friendly college scene I had just left. Most of the students, when asked, were not willing to work together on projects or help anyone else. I did start to work on a project with another classmate, but he soon quit meeting, and I found out later he had taken the work we had already done together and used it as his own. I got to know a fellow student named Mike Evans, who sat next to me in class as a result of alphabetical seating. Mike, an older student from Nevada, said he had been the pilot for casino owner Bill Harrah's private plane. Married and living in a rented house in San Francisco's Sunset District, he had come to Hastings to make a career change. Mike, a classy world traveler, was also a nice guy. He and his wife would invite me to dinner so I could occasionally have a home-cooked meal. I liked to listen to Mike's stories about traveling and seeing the world, something I also wanted to do. Mike introduced me to sake, the Japanese rice drink, served warm in very small cups. The first time, Mike warned me that a small amount could have a big effect, and I found he was right. I got light-headed and had to lie down on their couch for an hour.

Mike philosophized that most people never put romance in their own lives or the lives of those around them. He summed this up by his folksy admonition, "Never give someone a plant when you can buy them flowers." After law school, he returned to Nevada and became a county district attorney. While some other law school classmates seemed friendly enough, many were not. Some were older guys like Mike, hoping to change careers but worried they had made the wrong decision. The other group included younger students like me, except most had family members or friends who were lawyers. In law school, I saw a new kind of competition I hadn't experienced before. Some guys said they *had* to graduate and *had* to pass the bar exam, or they would embarrass their family and be disowned. Perhaps their dad or uncle practiced law, and failure would be devastating to their whole family. Many students admitted they didn't really want to be there. On the first day of law school, the dean announced to our class that half the students would fail and leave law school. This put a lot of pressure on everyone and ended the idea of helping out our fellow classmates.

My days were filled with stress from law school, anxiety from being a long way from home, and unease living in a completely different environment. I was lonely and nervous to the point of fear about my city life, especially while walking the dark streets and riding the bus at night. One night I stepped off the curb on Columbus Avenue and started to cross the street when a car pulled up to me. The passenger pointed a silver pistol at me and barked a warning to "get back on that fucking curb!" After that, I considered giving up law school altogether and moving back to Ohio. I was torn between wanting to leave and wanting to live up to Dad's admonition to "never give up" in life. I was the first in my family to go to graduate school and I wanted to succeed, but failing and leaving school was constantly on my mind. I told Duke about my homesickness. I said, "Duke, I don't mind the hard schoolwork, but this place isn't friendly at all."

"Don't worry, Ben," he said. "You have more going for you than most of them. We both came from small rural areas, so we don't need to act tough or rude." His talk helped me. The upside was that with no family history in law, I think my family already considered my going to law school a big accomplishment, so I wasn't under quite the same kind of pressure as many of my classmates.

My friend from Ohio, Dennis Searles, or "Redhead," as we called him in grade school, had also moved to San Francisco and worked as a CPA in the Financial District. One day he said, "Hey, Ben, a gal I know says she has a friend you might like to meet."

"Who is it?" I asked.

"Her name is Judi, but that's about all I know," he said. "I'll get her address."

A couple of days later, Dennis gave me the address, and I drove my recent car purchase to her apartment. I knocked on the door and a girl came to the door—pleasant but not what I was hoping for. "Judi?" I asked.

"No, I'm Sally. I'll go get her," the girl said.

Judi came to the door and said, "Hi, I'm Judi, and you must be Ben." She invited me into their apartment. "So, you're going to law school at Hastings," she continued. "That's really exciting."

I said, "Well, some days it's not so exciting, but stressful. How about you?"

"Well," she said, "I moved here to work as a model."

"That's exciting."

"Some days it's more stressful than exciting," she replied with a chuckle.

I laughed as she repeated what I had just said. I immediately felt as though I'd known her for days rather than minutes.

Judi was about my age, tall and thin, with brown hair and blue eyes. She reminded me of a young Audrey Hepburn with her looks and gentleness. She was the complete opposite of the hippie girls in the Haight. When we got together at night, she'd listen to my stories about growing up on our Ohio farm. She had grown up in a small Central California town I had never heard of.

I had little money, lots of ideas, and more than a few concerns about the future. This was in contrast to the guys Judi dated from the Financial District. They took her to dinner at expensive restaurants, and after she said goodnight to them, she often came by my Haight-Ashbury apartment. We would spend Sunday afternoons in Golden Gate Park or the marina walking and talking, just doing simple things, enjoying a brief escape from her modeling career and my law school studies. When I brought her to my apartment on Waller Street, she liked to be held and hugged, but I was very gentle and respectful of her feelings, thinking how fortunate I was to have her as a friend. Sometimes Judi and I went on dates together with Dennis and his friend Carol. We drove the English Ford across the Golden Gate Bridge during a heavy rainstorm. Dennis and Carol had to pull their feet up to the back seat to keep their shoes out of the standing water.

Judi and I talked about the Ohio farm on Zenobia Road where I'd lived until leaving for college. "How far is your farm from Cleveland?" she asked. I told her it was about an hour drive.

"I'd like to come visit you next summer in Ohio. Could I do that?"

"That'd be great," I said. I was surprised she would make the effort to visit and was already thinking about Mom and Dad's reaction.

On her way to New York that summer, as she had said she would, Judi stopped off in Cleveland. I met her at the airport, gave her a big hug, and headed to the parking lot and the old brown Pontiac. On the way to the farm, I stopped at a bar at the intersection of Route 20 and Quarry Road and bought a six-pack of beer. I drove to Chenango Road just north of our farm and stopped for a while to down a beer, thinking it would help me be a little less nervous when introducing Judi to Mom and Dad. As we drove up the gravel driveway to our house, Mom and Dad both came out to the front step to greet us. "Well, hello there," Mom said. "How was your trip here?"

"It was fine, but kind of long," Judi replied.

I got Judi's suitcase out of the car, and we went into the house through the kitchen door. Mom said, "I thought you might be hungry from the long trip and made some apple pie."

"That would be great," Judi said.

Even though she was tall and thin, she seemed happy eating Mom's sweets.

The next morning Mom fixed a breakfast of eggs and pancakes. Judi kept complimenting Mom about the food. After breakfast, Dad asked Judi if she would like to look around the farm. Judi said, "Sure, I'd like that." Dad walked with Judi and me from the house on the gravel driveway to the cow barn. Along the way we stopped to see the pigs and the chickens in their coops.

"How about getting up on the tractor?" I suggested.

"Yeah, I can do that," she said. The sight of the young girl from San Francisco sitting on Dad's Ford tractor still hangs in my mind.

Aside from the break of Judi's visit that summer, I worked long days and nights at two jobs. I spent my days at Bendix-Westing-house, a hot, noisy factory in Elyria that made truck air brakes, and at night I helped Dad finish the farmwork. Before I came home that summer, I had abandoned my English Ford on a San Francisco street where I parked it next to the curb with the key in the ignition. The car was not fit to drive all the way to Ohio, and having no place to park and no money to store it, I just left it on the street.

Before I returned to San Francisco later that summer, Dad paid Forrest Fletcher, one of the neighbors near our farm, $500 for a small, red, six-cylinder Pontiac Tempest that was parked in their front yard with a "FOR SALE" sign on it. The Tempest had no air-conditioning or radio. For the long drive back to California, Dad used his talent for practical solutions by wiring a portable battery-operated radio to the outside of the driver's side vent window. He tried to mount the radio inside, but the electrical charge from the spark plugs caused such loud static that it was impossible to hear anything else. With no air-conditioning, I had the windows open and could hear the music playing. At the time, only a few radio stations were available during the cross-country drive. I listened to one from Nashville and, as I drove farther west, another from Oklahoma City. On this second cross-country trip, I was alone and paid more attention to the countryside. Without having to listen to the nonstop-talking Jack, I also had time to think. The scenery and the roads hadn't really changed, but I had. I was not as fearful of what I would find as the first trip. Now that I had lived in the midst of Haight-Ashbury, I knew what to expect.

I also thought about the admonition from our dean only a couple of days after school started. "After this first year, about half of you will be gone, dropped out or flunked out, for whatever reason." I had made it through the first year and I was proud of myself, although I had a long way to go.

This second trip was slower, as I was the only driver. I stopped a couple of times and slept at a motor inn. At one motor inn the attendant was on the second floor, never came down, and took my money and gave me the room key by passing it down on a long stick.

"Where you headed?" she asked.

"California," I said sort of proudly.

"Well," she said, "I've never been there, but I don't want to go either."

"Why's that?" I asked.

She replied, "Seems like there's just hippies and problems."

"Yeah, I'm from Ohio, so I understand what you're saying, but California is my home for the time being." I retrieved the key from the stick and headed to a small nondescript room for the night.

During my second year of law school, Mom and Dad flew to California to visit my brothers Dale and Dan in Fresno. Dan then drove them to San Francisco to visit me. Parking in the nearest driveway Dan could find near my apartment with his car pulled forward as much as possible, the sharp rear tail fins of his maroon Chrysler New Yorker still stuck out past the curb into the street.

The Haight-Ashbury scene at that time, with its hippies, gays, and transvestites prancing around the streets and kissing each other openly, was not what my Ohio farm family was used to seeing. While Dan made a few sarcastic remarks, Mom and Dad never showed any negative reaction. After showing my family the Haight-Ashbury apartment, Dan drove us in his maroon Chrysler to a nice restaurant for dinner. It was a complete change from the skimpy meals I usually made for myself.

▶ THE TIMES THEY ARE A-CHANGIN'

I thought the best chronicle of the Haight-Ashbury era was Bob Dylan's 1964 song "The Times They Are a-Changin'." One day at school that same year, Duke said, "Hey, Ben, I got us a ride to see Bob Dylan tonight in San Jose."

"I'm in!" I said. We rode with some others to the Dylan concert at the San Jose Civic Auditorium. His unique voice, harmonica, and lyrics are still in my mind. *The times really are a-changin'*, I thought.

It occurred to me that Haight-Ashbury rose and fell in just a few years. This same time period represented the rise and fall of many political and cultural movements in America. It began about the time of the November 1963 assassination of President John F. Kennedy and ended about the time of the April 1968 assassination of Martin Luther King Jr. In this five-year period came the rise of the hippie culture, the 1967 Haight-Ashbury Summer of Love, and, in September of that year, the "Death of the Hippie" March and the ending of the era. During this period, opposition to the Vietnam War became more vocal and violent, as did political and cultural turmoil in the San Francisco Bay Area and the rest of the country.

Duke and I eventually left the neighborhood and rented a second-floor apartment, furnished with fancy Japanese-style furniture in the Castro District south of Market Street. Riding home from law school class one afternoon on the back of Duke's motorcycle, I saw a truck pull away from the curb next to our Castro District apartment. The back of the truck was stacked with what looked like our apartment's Japanese furniture. We found the apartment empty of the landlord's furniture as well as our two cheap beds and mattresses.

We tracked down our landlord at her apartment in the Tenderloin District and knocked on the door. She opened a small window in her door and talked through the hole, telling us in her near perfect, non-native English, "Get fuckin' lost."

Duke replied, "It's not fair; you can't do this. I prepaid all the rent." He had paid with a check from a Catholic charity from his hometown. "I have to get it back," he pleaded. After another round of profanity, the landlady explained that her boyfriend had stolen the furniture and she couldn't help us, then shut the peephole, ending our conversation and contact with her.

My first taste of the American justice system came when I filed a case, Ewell vs. Arselova, against the landlord in the San Francisco Small Claims Court to recover our lost beds, mattresses, and the prepaid rent.

The end result of this litigation mirrored what our tort professor, Dean Prosser, admonished us as first-year students. He posed the question, "You can sue the bishop of Boston for bastardy, but can you collect?" The answer in those days was clearly *no*. Now, it might be different.

I obtained a judgment but collected no money as our professor had warned. With our beds and rent money gone, we had to look for a new and less expensive furnished place to live. We decided to room with two other Hastings students to help share the cost. We found a three-story house on Noe Street, where we lived on the ground floor.

On the building's second floor directly above us was a flamenco dancer who practiced his fancy steps on a wood floor in his apartment almost every night. Members of the Bay Area Nudist Colony lived on the third floor. Just to be neighborly and breaking what must have been a solemn oath to their members upon joining the club, they allowed Duke and me to attend a meeting with our clothes on, while theirs were off. I felt nudity was more appropriate in the bedroom. By the end of law school, Duke had dropped out with failing grades and still worked in a parking garage, but we continued to room together at Noe Street.

I lived in the Noe Street house until the end of the school year and remained there until after graduation to study for and take the California Bar Exam. In June of 1966, Mom and Dad flew to California for my law school graduation ceremony held on the University of California, Berkeley campus. Dale and Dan were also there. Dan said, "Well, Benny, you're just what we need, another lawyer."

Dale, who was never sarcastic like Dan, said, "I'm really proud of you, Ben. You stuck with it, just like I thought you would."

Mom kept saying, "Honey, I'm so proud of you."

Dad, as usual, didn't say much except, "Son, I'm glad you made it."

Instead of returning to Ohio after graduation from law school, I stayed that summer to study for the California Bar Exam. Duke continued to live with us, still working at his nighttime garage attendant job. I worked all that summer to review each of the thirty-six subjects expected to be on the bar exam. I studied almost every night in a cubicle on an upper floor of the UC Medical Center complex on Parnassus Avenue in Haight-Ashbury. No one asked if I was a medical student. I just used the space and lived mostly on hot watery soup and soggy, premade, plastic-wrapped sandwiches from the medical center vending machines.

Most days, I also studied all night, including the day before of the bar exam. On the morning of the exam at six o'clock when the grocery store across from our apartment opened, I bought a box of powdered donuts, a pint of milk, and a bottle of cheap wine, and had some of all three. I headed off to the bar exam test site in my Pontiac Tempest with the pint of milk and the box of powdered donuts in my lap. The exam site was in an auditorium in downtown San Francisco. There were many strange reactions by the test takers that day. A few let out a sigh of resignation, and some ran out of the room and never returned. I couldn't type, so I had to write the essay questions in blue-lined colored booklets. With my poor handwriting, I'm not sure they could read my answers, and that was probably a good thing for me. The only thing that kept me somewhat calm about the whole exam process was the cheap wine I'd drunk that morning.

After the bar exam, I drove the red Pontiac Tempest to Fresno, parked it at my brother Dale's place, and flew back to Ohio to work the remaining days of summer.

After I moved away from San Francisco, I sometimes went back there on weekends to walk around the city, thinking about what had happened to me and the area during my time living there. I was asked, "Do you realize you were at ground zero in the 1960s?" I didn't think of it that way at the time. It was just another place to live, although completely different from anything I had known before or since.

In later years, Haight-Ashbury became trendy and commercial. The memory of the Grateful Dead lived on at the Ben and Jerry's ice cream store at the intersection of Haight and Ashbury, a half block from their original apartment. Patrons could order the Cherry Garcia flavor. Now an RCVA clothing store occupies the site just down from the Pink Dolphin, another trendy expensive clothing store. The former Safeway at the Golden Gate Park entrance is now a Whole Foods Market. Seventy-Two Central Avenue has a new coat of paint and probably more.

On a recent visit to Best Buy, I purchased Janis Joplin's album *18 Essential Songs* so I could try to relive some of the Haight-Ashbury era sounds with her distinctive screaming voice. The salesgirl at the checkout counter, who must have been born about thirty years after Joplin's death, looked over the CD jacket and song list. "Ya know," she said, "I just sang 'Piece of My Heart' on my way to work this morning." It impressed me that someone that age would know about and apparently appreciate a singer of the San

Francisco hippie era. I thought, *Some things never change.* For me, it was one more unusual experience that differed so much from my life on our Ohio farm, but it certainly fed my desire for adventure in my life. We all need adventures that expand our minds in order to better appreciate the world around us.

Chapter 7

LIFE
IN FRESNO

When I returned to Fresno from Ohio that summer, the Pontiac Tempest was covered with a thick dark brown layer of dust. The books and papers I'd left in the car were glued together from the hundred-degree heat. Dan had asked me to stay with him, so I moved the Pontiac from Dale's place in the Sunnyside area of town to Dan's North Delno Street home.

I had liked growing up on our Ohio farm and living in the country, and Fresno was country too, but different. Unlike the green of the Ohio countryside in summer, the hot, dry Fresno summers made the place look desolate. I felt different now about being in a rural area, thinking it would limit my opportunities and make adventure harder to attain. After listening to San Francisco Bay Area radio stations for the past four years, and then hearing a Fresno radio announcer give a "raisin drying report," I began to think I'd made a mistake moving to this city.

I knew the money I'd earned in Ohio that summer wouldn't last long in California, and my loan from the Producers Credit Association had been used up. I needed a job. After being in Fresno only a couple of weeks, I'd started job hunting by driving around town with Dan's telephone book on the front seat of my

Tempest, now cleaned up and drivable. This was well before the days of cell phones, so I would cover the telephone receiver at pay phones during my calls to muffle the sound of passing cars and trucks. I called several law offices listed in the "Attorneys" section of the phone book, but only one, Smith and Lawson, invited me to interview for a job. Located in downtown Fresno, I found the law firm on the fifth floor of a building with a large, rotating "G" on the top, advertising the Guarantee Savings and Loan Company. I was told the sign would change from green to red, depending on the day's temperature, and that day it was bright red. It must have been in the hundreds.

I entered the law firm and told the receptionist I had an appointment with Steve, one of the firm's lawyers, to see about a job. She showed me to his office. He was shorter than I and a little pudgy, with light brown hair. He wore a yellow shirt with slacks but no tie or coat. We shook hands, and I settled into the chair he directed me to in front of his desk. He asked where I was from.

"Ohio. I grew up on a farm there," I replied, adding, "I can already see that farms in Ohio are different from farms here." He didn't acknowledge my observation.

"Where did you go to college?" he asked.

I told him Miami University in southwestern Ohio and added that my three brothers also graduated from there.

"How did you get to California?" he asked.

"I came to California to go to law school."

"I mean, how did you get here?" he asked.

"Well, I answered an ad in the Cleveland paper looking for drivers," I replied.

I could feel the tension building in my body, as it seemed I was being grilled more than necessary. The truth was that I had never had a job interview. The construction work bosses couldn't care less about who you were and where you were from. Their only concern was whether you looked capable of doing the work. The only interview I'd ever had was before college graduation when I met with the Swift Meat Company. Since I was an Ohio farm boy, they thought I would fit nicely into their hiring plans. It was after that one and only meeting, when Swift Meat Company said I had a bright future with them in their pork department, that I decided the idea of law school looked pretty good.

"What law school?" Steve asked.

Trying to impress him, I answered with the full name, "The University of California Hastings College of Law in San Francisco."

"Well," he replied, "we're only looking for men from Stanford at this time, so we wouldn't really be interested in you. Sorry I can't help." He got up from his desk to show me the door.

I didn't know anything about Stanford, but I recalled a comment made by the father of my college friend Katie King. He had grumbled that Stanford was no match intellectually for the Eastern schools. Since he had been a lawyer and member of the New York Bar Association at the time, I figured he must know something about the standards of various law schools. Over the years, I've encountered people always putting down the other guy's school, background, or profession. I never thought much about school or alumni loyalties. They didn't seem that important to me, either then or now. I never spent time concerned about the other guy, what he had or hadn't done or was planning to do. I had the same law degree as all other California law school graduates, and if I passed the bar exam, I'd have the same license to practice as all the other California lawyers, including Steve from Stanford, who had turned me down. I didn't really care what he thought about Hastings. But I did walk away needing to make more phone calls.

Not having any success calling the private firms, I went by the Fresno County District Attorney's Office to see about a job. The deputy district attorney in charge of hiring was friendly but said the office didn't have any openings at the time. He suggested that I speak with Jim Thuesen, an attorney in private practice who had previously been the Fresno County District Attorney. I had never heard of him.

"Maybe he can help you," the deputy said. "Here's his address." He suggested I walk over to his nearby office to speak with him while I was still in downtown Fresno.

Walking past the empty receptionist's desk in Thuesen's tenth-floor office in the Security Bank Building, I heard the sound of a radio playing in the back. I found an elderly man listening to a San Francisco Giants baseball game with both legs stretched out on top of his desk, leaning back in a swivel chair with his arms folded behind his head. At the door of the office, I stuck my head in, and he motioned for me to come in and take a seat.

"I'm Jim," he said. "They called over here and said you'd be coming." He spoke in an unusually loud voice to be heard over the sound of the radio. He had short-cropped, gray-and-white hair and a smile showing big teeth, like a picture of Teddy Roosevelt. He had a giggly laugh that reminded me of Elmer, our neighbor on Zenobia Road.

"I'll look . . ." he started to say, but he stopped suddenly in mid-sentence to concentrate on the announcer describing a line drive hit to the outfield. Then he finished his sentence, "I'll look around for something; maybe I can help you out. Give me a phone number." I gave him my bother Dan's home phone number.

A couple of days later, the phone rang at Dan's home and my sister-in-law handed it to me. Thuesen was on the line. "I found something," he said. "It's in a law office, but you're not gonna like the boss, and it ain't much of a job at four hundred dollars a month. Do you want it?"

Impulsively and without asking questions, I told him I'd take the job. Neglecting to inquire about details was consistent with my approach to most things. I tended to jump quickly without hesitation to catch any opportunity coming my way and work out any issues later.

I showed up the following day on the fourth floor of the same building as Thuesen's office and asked to see Harold Prentice, the attorney Thuesen had set me up with. The receptionist showed me to his office and told me to take a seat. The man behind the desk had an unusually large head, thick black hair with gray streaks, and bushy sideburns. He seemed to be talking on two phones to two different people at the same time, all the while giving instructions to his secretary. As I sat in front of his desk, he looked at me and then winked as he spoke to the caller on one receiver.

I overheard him say to the caller on one phone, "I'm going all the way to try this case. Your client's a fraud; his injuries are nothing. I have more pain in one minute than he'll have the rest of his life. I won't pay over fifty thousand to settle this case."

I thought he must have been talking to an attorney for an injured plaintiff in a lawsuit.

On the other phone in the other ear, he seemed to be talking to a representative of the defendant in the same lawsuit. Cupping his hand over the telephone receiver so the first caller couldn't hear, he told the second caller, "This is one of the worst injury cases I've ever seen. I need a two-hundred-thousand-dollar authority from you to try and get out of this case. I'll be a hero if I can get this settled for two hundred thousand."

Then he went back to the first caller. "All right, you have really beaten me down. I'll give you exactly what you want, a hundred grand. Don't forget I've gone out on a limb for you."

Then he went back to the second person on the other phone, saying, "He wanted two hundred thousand, but I made him take a hundred grand. You really owe me on this one."

After both conversations had ended and the telephone receivers put back in place, he smiled and said to me, "Young man, that's the way to settle a case."

I had a lot more to learn before I could put on that kind of performance. I thought back to Jim Thuesen's admonishment that I might not like the new boss. I had an uneasy feeling at that moment, but I couldn't articulate it even to myself.

The receptionist showed me to a small office with a bare wooden desk, one chair, one window, and a shelf with some books. This was my first office job. Except for the Ohio Bendix-Westinghouse factory, I had always worked outdoors, either on the farm or in construction. Seated at my desk, I wanted to feel what it must be like to be a lawyer. Now I can see that at the time, I was feeling more important than I should have since I hadn't been sworn in as an attorney or even received my bar exam results.

A few weeks later, I received a letter in an envelope marked "The State Bar of California" with a San Francisco return address delivered to Dan's house, as I was using his address to receive mail. Dan said, "Hey, Ben, you have a letter from the state bar. You should come by the house and see what it says."

When I got to Dan's, I thought, *What if I failed the bar? What would they say about me at my new job?* I realized that was a possibility, but with my hand actually a little shaky, I opened the letter and saw the words, "Congratulations, you have successfully passed the California State Bar Exam." I said, "Dan, come look at this."

He read over the letter and said, "Well, it's about time you started earning a real living."

After I received notice that I'd passed the bar exam, I went to San Francisco to be sworn in as an attorney.

A few days afterward, I was pleased when Prentice assigned me my first case, representing a landlord who happened to be a family friend of his. Our client, the plaintiff in the case, owned an apartment building and claimed the defendant, one of his tenants, owed for the damage to the apartment's window curtains caused by the tenant's dog. It wasn't much of a case and could have been settled out of court, but Prentice wanted to prove a point to his client and not appear weak. Locating a book on trial procedure in the Fresno County Law Library, I read the chapter on how to address the court and submit evidence, something I probably should have learned more about in law school. On the date set for trial, I showed up at the courthouse, very nervous about the upcoming trial. I had woken up a couple of times during the night, drunk some brandy, and tried to go back to sleep.

That morning I walked toward the county courthouse and wondered if they would be able to smell the alcohol on my breath, but it was too late to worry about that. As the judge entered the courtroom, I stood up and the bailiff announced court was in session and called the name of the case. The judge asked, "Is the plaintiff ready?"

"Ready, Your Honor," I said, responding in a voice that sounded like I had actually done this before. I proceeded to present my case the way I had read about at the law library.

I called the apartment manager to the stand. He described the torn curtains and the estimated damaged caused by the defendant's dog. The defendant's attorney proceeded to submit pictures of the tenant's apartment furniture, including a coffee table and couch against the opposite wall away from the torn curtains. The bottom of the damaged curtains hung at least four feet above the floor. The defendant testified that his small dog couldn't have caused the curtain damage and that the curtains were old and cheap to start with and falling apart from age. The defendant's attorney then introduced a picture of his client's very small dog. After listening to the evidence, the judge adjourned the court, saying he would announce his decision shortly and left the courtroom. I thought, *I'm sure this will be a win for me, and my client and Prentice will be pleased.*

About fifteen minutes later, the judge returned to the courtroom, and the bailiff asked everyone to rise and then, after the judge was seated, to be seated.

"Mr. Ewell, the court will take judicial notice of the small size of the dog, and its inability to reach high enough to chew up the curtains. Judgment in favor of the defendant."

I did not look forward to my walk back to the office to tell Prentice about losing my first case involving his friend. Prentice projected an aura of never losing at anything in life. Then it hit me. If the couch against the other wall had been in place on the wall underneath the window with the curtains, the dog could have run along the top of the couch and chewed the curtains. It was too late; the case was over. When I gave Prentice the news about the verdict, he said, "You should never have lost." He never discussed the matter with me again.

This incident reminded me of an important lesson for all of us: never assume what an outcome might be. It was a lesson I first learned as a boy, when raising chickens for the purpose of selling them and earning some money. Dad gave me twenty eggs to start my little business. To me, all the eggs looked the same. I kept them warm under a heat lamp, ready to have twenty chicks I could raise and sell. After about three weeks, I found out that only seventeen eggs had little chicks inside. As Dad reminded me afterward, "You counted them before they hatched."

▶ TAKING CARE OF BUSINESS

While I was still in law school, my brother Dan, a CPA by profession, had gotten involved in farming, with the idea of growing and selling pistachio trees. In the late 1960s, cotton was king in the flat open lands of western Fresno County, while eastern Fresno County grew grapes, citrus, and tree fruit. No pistachio trees grew in either area. I learned that pistachio trees had not been grown commercially in the United States because of trouble raising and transplanting the seedlings. Instead of flood irrigation, with huge amounts of water released down the furrows of a flat field, pistachios grew in desertlike conditions on rolling terrain, needing less water and best suited for a type of irrigation system with small drip emitters installed on top of the ground. Dan worked with a company to buy small, plastic tubular lines and emitter heads for an irrigation system to water the trees. The local farmers, suspicious of growing exotic nut trees like pistachios, required a lot of convincing to buy and plant the first trees.

Dan's involvement had started when he met Don Howard, an orange tree nurseryman. Dan and Don asked me to form a new company and said I could own a portion in exchange for my legal services. We expected to start and maintain this small business to supplement the income Dan earned from accounting and I from law.

At the time, only a few pistachio trees existed in the entire state of California, and none in the rest of the country. Pistachio nuts, usually of poor quality and imported from Iran at the time, had their shells dyed red to cover blemishes. Conditions for importing pistachios from the Middle East grew worse as a result of conflicts in that part of the world that culminated in the Iran hostage crisis. The importation of nuts to the United States from Iran eventually stopped completely, and a US domestic market was needed to replace the lost imports. We found this was our niche in the agriculture business.

We purchased the seeds needed to grow the first pistachio plants from two Armenian rug dealer brothers in San Francisco who owned a few trees in the Sacramento area. We met them at their San Francisco rug store to buy seeds. I still recall haggling with the two brothers, surrounded by the expensive colorful displayed rugs in their Union Square store in the heart of the city's shopping district. Customers who overheard our conversations surely thought our loud negotiations involved something much more sinister than pistachio seeds.

Dan and I set up a tree nursery in a large vacant area at the back of his Delno Street house in Fresno. I wasn't sure if Dan owned the adjacent lot, and neither he nor I inquired about it. Trucks rumbled through Dan's neighborhood, delivering soil and mulch. Leaving the law office at the end of the day, I would drive to Dan's house to water and care for the pistachio seedlings. I felt a little bit like I was still on the farm. In the first year, we were able to grow several dozen plants while Dan tried to convince farmers to buy and plant our small seedlings.

As the attorney for the business, I typed up papers to form the Pistachio Growers Association, the Root Creek Irrigation Company, Great Western Nurseries, and a farm management company, all of which sounded important but at the time consisted of just Dan, Don Howard, and I. Years later, the Growers Association would represent several hundred thousand acres of pistachio plantings throughout California. The nursery grew too large for Dan's backyard and was moved to a location in nearby Madera County where Don had been growing orange trees for sale. As Dan's younger brother, I had always worked in his shadow and didn't have the passion for business that he clearly had. Making money didn't seem as important to me as it was to Dan. Dan and I got along really well, but in business matters he could be tough as nails. One day he said, "Ben, you should get out of the law practice; you're never going to make a lot of money with a bunch of guys who want to play golf or tennis all the time. I know what it's like from my days in the Smith and Jones accounting firm."

SUNDAY AFTERNOONS AND OTHER TIMES REMEMBERED

I replied, "Yeah, I know you're probably right, but I worked hard to get here."

"Well," he said, "remember what I said, because you'll find out one day that I'm right."

About five years after the start of the pistachio venture, Dan was approached to sell our entire pistachio business and began negotiating with a Florida-based company traded on the American Stock Exchange. The company described itself as the largest citrus grower in the United States, owning thousands of acres of orange trees in Florida. The negotiations took place mostly in Miami, requiring constant cross-country trips by Dan and me.

With the sales agreement in place, I thought financial success was just around the corner. We transferred our company, properties, and the pistachio business we'd worked hard to start to the Florida company in exchange for its company stock and a promise of large future profit sharing. A few months after closing the transaction, we learned the US Securities and Exchange Commission had filed a complaint against the Florida company for misleading investors in its Florida orange grove business. We had been drawn into something that I thought could ruin my legal career and any reputation I might have in the Fresno community. We had been naive as well as greedy to think we could easily cash in with this big company.

Two brothers who, according to the SEC allegations, controlled the Florida company, had allegedly flown investors to Florida to see their investments and represented to multiple investors that each owned the same piece of citrus orchard.

The first brother, Jared, seemed to be the brains of their business empire and said he knew little about the company field operations, leaving that to his brother, Jason, who he said liked to wander in the orchards and "talk to the trees."

Jared talked about his sales approach by explaining his "red car" theory. "When someone wants to buy a red car, you have to tell them that the red car is already spoken for but that there is a real nice blue car available. Then when you see the customer's disappointed face, you tell the customer, just a minute, let me see what I can do, and head off to the manager's office. Upon return-ing, you tell the customer you're going to do him a favor and that the red car can still be theirs, but it'll cost them more money . . ."

"Did you get that?" he said to me.

"Yeah, I did," I replied, trying to absorb what he had just said. First was the deception that I often associated with salespeople. Second was the human tendency to want and strive for the things we can't have; the external denial of our own desire creates our increased interest in something, and even a requirement to pay extra doesn't always discourage us.

We hired Manuel F. Cohen, a Washington, DC, power attor-ney and the former chairman of the Securities and Exchange Commission in the Kennedy and Johnson administrations, with many contacts and a very high hourly billing rate, to help us sort out our problems with the Florida company.

On our behalf, Cohen painted a picture to the staff of the Securities and Exchange Commission, many of whom had proba-bly worked for him when he was chairman, that as farm boys from Fresno, we had in good faith transferred our properties and inter-ests to a company now in trouble through no fault of our own, and we just wanted our property and our business back.

In the end, to our great relief, Cohen succeeded. Our prior sale transaction was unwound, and the pistachio business and property was returned to us.

After resolving this mess, I got out of the pistachio business and returned to concentrating on my law practice. At this point, I felt that business life, at least this one, just wasn't for me. Dan and Don Howard stayed with it, continuing to grow the nursery business, land development, and farming to a very large operation. It takes time to realize that some things we're involved in—a job, a career, or a relationship—aren't serving us and we should probably do something else. It takes courage to follow our intuition and make a change. Doing business with Dan made me realize not only how very strong our family ties were but also how different our personalities and interests were. I didn't have the same interest in making money, and I needed to get out from Dan's shadow, even if that meant losing out financially.

The second case assigned to me at the Prentice law office was the daughter of one of Prentice's family friends, a woman named Kathy who wanted a divorce. Before the passage of no-fault divorce laws, California required the party seeking the divorce to prove fault, such as adultery, on the part of the other spouse.

Kathy was dark haired, attractive, and quite tall. She appeared to be about my age, in her mid-twenties. She arrived for her appointment carrying a brown paper bag. After a brief discussion, she pulled out what she described as bedsheets slept on by her husband and his girlfriend. I tried not to look too surprised. After taking notes on her background, marriage, and information necessary to file divorce papers, she asked me if I was single and whether I had a girlfriend.

"Yes, I'm single, and no, I don't really have a girlfriend. I haven't been in Fresno very long. I've gone out a few times and met some gals, but nothing serious."

"Why don't you and I go out?" she asked.

"No," I said. "I can't date someone I'm representing in a divorce."

"What if you weren't representing me?"

"That might be different," I replied.

"Well, let me think about it. I'll call back for another appointment," she said, ending our conversation.

Kathy did call a couple of days later. When I got on the line she said, "I thought about it."

"About what?" I asked.

"I'm getting a different lawyer," she replied, and proceeded to tell me where to meet her that week. The office lost a client, but I found a good friend. Kathy and I saw each other off and on for several months. She was funny, adventurous, and philosophical.

When we rented a cabin in Yosemite National Park one weekend, she noticed me looking over her shoulder at a framed painting above our bed. The painting had the phrase "Consider the Lilies" against a background field of flowers with the biblical reference Luke 12:27. She mentioned, "It's a beautiful saying."

Arriving home that weekend, I looked up the Bible verse and its message: the beauty of a flower in nature is greater than all the glory of Solomon. That thought would stay with me over the years as my appreciation for the beauty of nature and the world around me continued to grow. As a young boy on our farm, I liked to walk in our woods and look at the different plants and flowers; then I would check out books from the library and try to identify them. I collected the leaves of the beech, maple, oak, walnut, hickory, and ash trees and pressed them into hot wax to preserve them. As time went on, I liked to remember those simple ways that I had enjoyed life. I thought about how growing up on the farm has stayed with me. I thought I might have the best of two worlds, one where I lived and the other in my thoughts. One life in the fast-moving, always eventful California, and the memories of a much slower and, in its own way, equally beautiful Ohio. I didn't really want to return to Ohio to live, but I liked to recall my earlier life there.

About four years after passing the bar, I left the Prentice office and accepted a position in a large Fresno law firm. I tried to adjust to the relationships and politics of a large office but never became comfortable in the corporate setting. As Dan had predicted, fellow lawyers could be jealous; even though our pistachio business was a paying client of the law firm, I could sense standoffishness when I returned from trips to Florida, or their wives would resent lawyers who might be better compensated than their husbands. Still single, I often showed up at law firm events with dates who were immediately given the once-over from my colleagues' wives.

I tried not to get involved in any of these office conflicts. I worked mostly on business litigation, which I didn't like, and then business transactions, which I liked only a little more. I kept thinking I'd rather be putting my own transactions together instead of working on someone else's projects.

One day, a partner in the firm stuck his head in the door of my office.

"Ewell," he said. "You were born on a farm, right?"

"Yeah, in Ohio. Why do you want to know?"

"Well, we need to have you interview for a general counsel position to represent the Kings River Water Association. This would be a very big client for the firm."

"What do they do?"

"Well, it has to do with water, and you're a farm boy, aren't you?" he continued.

"Yeah, but in Ohio, it just rains. I don't know anything about irrigation."

As I had when I prepared for my first trial, I went to the county law library and looked up material on the Kings River and California water rights.

I interviewed for the general counsel position and was selected to represent an organization that soon became my biggest client. The people I met and worked with became a major part of my life and legal career. I liked the work with family farming interests, the history that went with the water issues, and the political involvement. Starting with this one client, I began to specialize in water law. It suited me better than my previous work because it was more about people, politics, and relationships, and less about research and law books.

The Kings River in central California provided irrigation water to over a million acres of property with farms served ranging from a few to thousands of acres in size.

California water politics really hadn't changed much since the 1800s, and the battles over water continued among competing interests. Strongly held views about who owned the water and how much they owned became a solid foundation for disputes that continue to this day. Farming on this scale was unlike anything I had seen in Ohio. There were corporate jets and Washington lobbyists. As part of my job as a representative for water interests, I testified before Congress on more than one occasion.

I soon got other large water-related clients as my business expanded. I thought back to a question asked of me by one of the interviewers during the Kings River Water Association General Counsel selection process: "Do you have any other water clients?"

I answered, "No, but if I'm selected, I'm sure I'll get others."

This prediction turned out to be true. My time at the large firm ended after a series of disputes with one particular partner. Finally, I left and started my own law office, something I should have done much earlier. Since I was the only lawyer in the firm with clients in the water business, they all left and followed me to my new firm.

▶ THE SOCIAL SCENE

I was in my early twenties and needed a social life. Because there were not many women my age in the law profession, I started going out to a couple of Fresno nightspots. But even if I did meet someone, I couldn't really take them back to Dan's house with my sister-in-law and Dan's two boys there, so I started looking for my own place to live. I moved out of Dan's house into a second-floor studio apartment I found for rent on San Pablo Street in a poorer part of Fresno. My one-room studio with a bed, kitchenette, and bathroom cost seventy-five dollars a month, the same rent Duke and I had paid at 72 Central Avenue in Haight-Ashbury.

A few nights after moving into the San Pablo apartment, a loud explosion woke me in the middle of the night. In the morning, the two girls in the apartment across the hall showed me where a random shotgun blast had blown a hole in their front door. They had just moved from Dallas and now seemed uncertain about their new hometown.

I was finally earning decent money and began going out on the town and drinking at night. I was in my twenties and going through a phase. I didn't want to settle down or date just one woman, especially after the daily grind of my law school years when I lacked the freedom to have a good time. The relationships with the gals I did meet usually ended after one or two dates, as one or both of us became interested in someone else.

These women were a diverse group. One took time to pray before becoming intimate; others included a sweet bank teller, a TWA stewardess in Jamaica, and a gal from Miami who came to Fresno to visit me. I still recall the auburn-haired girl from Los Angeles who served as maid of honor in my best friend's wedding. When we were introduced, she asked, "Are you the best man?"

"I'm pretty sure I'm one of the better ones," I said. In the coming months, we took turns meeting in Los Angeles and Fresno.

No one at the Prentice office ever mentioned that Kathy had found another attorney, assuming, I'm sure, that she wasn't sold on me being her lawyer. Like a lot of things in life, the secrecy around our relationship made it even more appealing.

Several months after meeting and dating Kathy, her younger

sister Margaret called me at the office. "Hey, what are you doing? This is Margaret, you know, Kathy's sister."

"Yes, I know who you are," I said.

She suggested we get together sometime.

"What about your sister?"

"She's all tied up with her divorce, and I understand you haven't seen her for quite a while anyway," she said.

She had a point, though I never found out if this was her way of getting back at her older sister for some slight. Margaret was quiet, moody, and thoughtful, quite different than Kathy, whom, I later learned, she had not initially told about our relationship. Eventually, Margaret left Fresno and moved to San Francisco, where I spent several weekends with her. Always sleeping on a waterbed, she tried, with very little success, to teach me how to enjoy the comfort of each other in a device that sloshed around all night.

► THE UGLY AMERICANS

When I was twenty-nine, a couple of my friends suggested we travel to Europe together. I had been to different resorts in Acapulco, Jamaica, and Hawaii with friends, but I'd never been to Europe. The European trip became a highlight of my world travels. All in our late twenties, we celebrated my thirtieth birthday at a restaurant in Paris. Besides me, the three other travelers included Ward Kimble, a six-foot-four stockbroker in Fresno and one of the funniest people I have ever known. His father was a Fresno attorney and his mother a descendent of a wealthy California pioneer family. Next was George Baker, a newspaper reporter and later executive editor of the *Fresno Bee* whom I first met when he was the newspaper's political reporter. George, with his sometime unkempt looks, constant coffee drinking, and often cynical attitude, looked and acted the part of a typical newsman. Baker's friend Ed Scripps from their college days together at Berkeley was the fourth traveler. I had not met him before our trip, but Scripps, the son of the Scripps newspaper chain owner, was overweight, and Kimble never stopped reminding him that he looked like an ugly American. This was a diverse group of friends, but we had fun and got along reasonably well, laughing at each other and other people we met. All the beer we drank did even more to improve our good humor.

Our first stop was Copenhagen. Because it was my first time in Europe, seeing live shows featuring nude men and women engaging in sex in front of us at a local nightclub took some getting used to. I had never seen prostitutes sitting by open windows as they did in Amsterdam's red-light district trying to entice prospective customers inside. I did my best to act like this was all fairly normal. My Midwestern upbringing where sex was hidden and rarely discussed reflected my overall attitude. In America, I thought of prostitutes hanging out on street corners in bad neighborhoods, but in Amsterdam, sitting in windows on display and promoting sex seemed to be considered business as usual.

After Copenhagen the four of us traveled to Paris. We eventually split up, and Scripps headed to London to visit a school he'd attended, Baker and Kimble traveled to Spain, and I rode the train by myself through Switzerland, Germany, and Austria, and then took flights to Italy, Spain, and Portugal.

Before leaving Paris, we decided to meet three weeks later in the coastal resort city of Estoril, Portugal, complete with its casino and tuxedo-wearing card dealers. Once there, Kimble met the casino requirements of wearing a tie by putting one around his neck with the longest part almost to the ground, a style he copied from the outfit worn by the comedian Professor Irwin Corey. With his cowboy boots and loud talk, he looked about as American as possible and told everyone he was from Texas and very rich. There was some actual truth to the rich part. Ward treated both friends and strangers the same with funny but sarcastic comments. I think that underneath all of the bravado he wanted acceptance. A typical comment of Ward's after a tragedy in our family was, "Ben, if you didn't have bad luck, you wouldn't have any luck at all." His comment was hurtful, but I think the barrier he had built around himself made it difficult for him to express feelings of concern and comfort to another person. I believe he was trying to acknowledge my rough times and bad luck but didn't know how to say so without making a joke.

That trip was in 1971, and America was engaged in the Cold War with the Soviet Bloc. In Austria, soldiers patrolled the train station when I arrived alone late at night. I took a Mercedes taxi through the streets of Vienna with opera playing on the radio and a non-English-speaking driver. I grew concerned as the taxi went farther into what seemed a dark, rough part of the city. Stopping finally under a train trestle, the driver motioned to an older ramshackle building indicating I should get out.

"Here?" I asked. "Do they have a room here?"

I didn't know for sure how much English the driver understood, but he nodded his head indicating yes and laughed.

When I knocked on the door of the run-down building, an older lady answered the door. She looked down at my suitcase, back to my eyes, and motioned for me to enter. We walked down the hallway to a room where several younger women in high heels and fancy dresses stood around, talking and smoking. The room became silent as the women stopped, turned, and looked at me. The older lady spoke to them, but I couldn't understand the language. They all laughed. One of the ladies stepped forward and said in broken English, "You vant a room, but you don't vant us, yes?"

"Yeah, I guess that's right," I replied, not knowing if anyone understood me and being more concerned with my safety that night than the women in the house. I had been dropped off at a whorehouse. After more broken English and hand signals, the older lady understood I wanted a room and not the women. I slept only a little that night, fully dressed, on a torn, stained mattress with no bedding in a small, foul-smelling, second-floor room. I left very early the next morning, wondering why the taxi driver had assumed this was what I wanted. Or had he been playing a joke on a young American guy? I never knew for sure. We tend to be suspicious of others who speak a different language, uncertain about what they actually understand about us. We think the worst of others who are different from us when we should take just the opposite approach, at least until we have reason to think otherwise.

▶ THE POLITICAL SCENE

After arriving home from the European trip, my life took another direction. With encouragement from Mike Cardenas, a friend and Fresno CPA, I started to get involved in politics, something I didn't know much about. I attended a meeting of the Fresno County Young Republicans. Maybe there was a shortage of other willing people, but not long afterward, I was elected chairman of the county organization and later to a position on the county Republican Central Committee. While it was a low-level position on the political scale, I still felt I had some bragging rights, thinking I might get even more involved.

I did stay involved, chairing Evelle Younger's Fresno-area campaign for California State Attorney General. He was well known in Southern California as the Los Angeles County District Attorney but not in central California. Younger wanted to organize a campaign in the Central Valley where he had little name recognition. A former FBI Agent, Younger came across as a nice guy with a solemn, humorless personality and the distinct look of law enforcement. I organized a breakfast fundraiser for Younger with Fresno lawyers and businessmen to raise money for his campaign. Before the event, I studied the names of about twenty-five people who had replied to my invitation indicating they would attend. I memorized their names so I could introduce them to the candidate. Standing at the end of a long table at the breakfast fundraiser at the Fresno Downtown Club, I went up and down both sides recalling each of their names and introduced each of the attendees to Younger. In everyday social and business settings, people like to be recognized and hear their name, and I am no different. In politics, it is even more important. Younger won the race for attorney general and four years later won a second term.

For helping him out, he appointed me to the California Council on Criminal Justice and Law Reform, which was my first political appointment. It was a more formal version of my getting the Ohio road crew job because the attorney I asked for that job had been chairman of the local Ohio Republican Party. I was one of only two non–law enforcement members on the council, and I felt out of place. I had never practiced criminal law and didn't think I wanted to. I didn't assert myself or try to take charge; I just attended the meetings, listening and learning about all kinds of crime-fighting hardware. Our job involved doling out government grants to law enforcement agencies with relatively little background study or common sense. The grant requests were almost always for equipment like helicopters, armored vehicles, or high-powered weapons. I thought of this as big toys for grown men.

In 1978, the last year of his second term as attorney general, Younger ran for governor of California against Jerry Brown, the son of the previous California governor. I served as Central Valley area chairman for Younger's campaign, helping to organize fundraisers and giving campaign speeches on behalf of the candidate. When he came through Fresno, he would often have his driver park his state car next to the Guarantee Savings Building in downtown Fresno and take the elevator to my fourth-floor office. A couple of times he stayed overnight at our home, and we made breakfast for him before he left for his appointments. His prospects seemed really good, and I told him so. California had a history of attorneys general successfully seeking the office of governor, but not this time. I don't think Younger ever lived down a radio spot run by the Brown campaign that played Hawaiian music in the background to emphasize that Younger, while taking a well-deserved break, had been on the beach in Oahu unconcerned about the state while his opponent stayed home, promoting an image of working hard for the people.

Younger's running mate in the campaign for governor was Mike Curb, a songwriter and record producer from Los Angeles. He won the lieutenant governor position, even though Younger lost the race for governor. I got to know Curb during the campaign, went to his political events, and visited him at his Los Angeles home in the hills above the city. The walls were lined with awards and memorabilia from his songwriting and record-producing career. I learned that Curb first achieved fame at age nineteen when, as a student at San Fernando College, he wrote "You Meet the Nicest People on a Honda," which the motor company purchased and selected for its ad campaign. In checking his background, I also learned that during his career he had composed or supervised over fifty motion picture soundtracks and written over four hundred songs.

I liked the excitement of meeting the various Hollywood types Curb surrounded himself with, like Casey Kasem of the weekly *American Top 40* radio program among others he had invited to a party at Elvis Presley's former home in Beverly Hills, which had unusual decor. All the walls were painted black, including the living room where singer Glen Campbell performed for us. I felt that I was really getting away from my Ohio farm roots. We are often intrigued by another lifestyle, especially one markedly different from our own. Usually after seeing some of the glimmer of another life, we welcome getting back to our own, and that is what happened to me.

Curb ran for governor four years later, and I was his Central California campaign chairman. This meant setting up appearances for Curb with local personalities and arranging fundraisers. Curb was defeated in the primary election by George Deukmejian, who ran a radio ad against him featuring a man singing in a falsetto voice, which they claimed was actually Curb sometime earlier in his musical career. After leaving politics, Curb gained huge success in the songwriting and recording industry.

My involvement in the various campaigns and meeting the diverse mix of people in politics allowed me to get even further away from the farm and the rural past I had known growing up in Ohio. Other campaigns followed, and when President Ford ran for election to a full term against Jimmy Carter, I served as Ford's cochairman in the Central Valley, which gave me the opportunity to meet and have lunch with him. My guest at the San Francisco lunch was Mary Jane Cavanaugh, a Minnesota transplant who helped me on my political campaign events and the farming business with my brother Dan. Ford, born in Nebraska and raised in Michigan, talked and acted like the Midwestern folks I had known my whole life. Even though he had been a star college football star, he seemed a little clumsy and not too inspiring when he spoke. Thinking I might run for public office myself at some point, I stayed involved and came to believe that while some had little regard for politics and the people involved, I thought of it as really no different from society in general. Some people had the best intentions, and others just the opposite.

I met George Herbert Walker Bush before he became the

forty-first president as he promoted other politicians before his own win. He was friendly and easily approachable but without much personality, which I thought became clear when he served his single term as president.

I helped out in Ronald Reagan's 1980 election and accepted an invitation to attend his inauguration. During the swearing-in ceremony, I stood in front of the US Capitol on a very cold January day along with thousands of others. I felt a tingle inside recalling a similar feeling years earlier in my childhood days watching the flag go by in the Spirit of '76 March on the Fourth of July from Grandma's house in Rochester, Ohio, or watching General Eisenhower speak from the rear of his campaign train.

Shortly after the Reagan inauguration, Mike Cardenas, who had earlier encouraged me to get involved in Fresno-area political campaigns, was appointed by President Reagan to head the Small Business Administration in Washington, DC. Mike mentioned to me later that he had met with the president on the morning of March 30, 1981, just before Reagan was shot. After his appointment, Mike asked me to chair the SBA's National Advisory Council. He had been told by the Reagan administration that the president intended to make the small business sector of the economy a major part of his presidency, believing that small businesses created most of the new jobs.

An envelope with the simple words *THE WHITE HOUSE* in the upper left-hand corner arrived at my law office. Inside was a request to meet with President Reagan at an afternoon White House reception for the advisory council of the SBA. Included was a note from the Secret Service requesting my social security number and my date and place of birth for the background check and security clearance.

My role as chairman of the SBA advisory council resulted in several visits to the White House and meetings with President

Reagan and other cabinet members. Each time, we traveled from our Washington hotel to the White House in a government van and entered through the diplomatic entrance. Inside that entrance was the diplomats' reception room with its floor-to-ceiling wall coverings depicting scenes of American history. This all seemed a long way from my days on the Ohio farm and my life in Haight-Ashbury among the hippies. Once again, I considered how sometimes we can be more comfortable than we would have expected when confronted with a unique and exciting opportunity. We have to learn to peel back the outer veneer of the event and find common ground with those involved.

The afternoon White House reception in the foyer off the North Portico entrance of the White House included US Attorney General Ed Meese and several other cabinet officials. As I stood near President Reagan, a US marine in full dress uniform with white gloved hands stepped forward and asked, "May I have your name? I want to introduce you to the president."

"Sure," I said. "I'm Ben Ewell from Fresno, California."

The marine then turned to Reagan. "Mr. President, let me introduce Mr. Ben Ewell of Fresno, California."

"Hello, Mr. President," I said, and then added, "I'm from your home state of California."

Whether you agreed with the president's policies or not, his reaction at that moment confirmed what others had written about his ability to put you at ease. He smiled, shook my hand, and began the conversation by saying, "I've been reading about the Fresno weather. I understand you've been having heavy winter rains this year." Reagan, as we often saw in photos of the day, was smiling while he shook my hand.

During another meeting with President Reagan in the Roosevelt Room of the White House, next to the Oval Office, I studied the Nobel Peace Prize medal displayed there in a glass container on the mantel. I researched it and found the medal had been awarded in 1906 to Teddy Roosevelt for his efforts in ending the Russo-Japanese War. I had heard so much about the Nobel Prize and couldn't quite believe it was in front of me.

At yet another visit to the White House, I attended a state visit on the White House lawn with President and Mrs. Reagan and experienced firsthand the ear-splitting sound of the cannon salute for the King of Nepal. Returning to Fresno and my law office after the Washington trips, I sensed jealousy on the part of the other lawyers in the firm about my travels, so I kept quiet about the presidential visits so as not to appear to be bragging. I learned the preferable use of an attorney's spare time was playing golf or tennis, not meeting with the president at the White House or building a farming company. I kept up in my involvement in the Fresno social scene, but I also followed Mom's approach to life and continued to be involved in numerous community organizations and political activities for many years.

▶ MOVING ON IN LIFE

A time came when Fresno dating and nightlife began to lose its appeal, and I thought I should settle down. One night when dining with my friend Ward Kimble, three gals seated at another table kept looking our way, or at least I thought they did. After dinner, Ward and I passed by their table and started up a conversation. They had finished dinner and were also starting to leave. We walked with them out to the lobby and continued talking on our way to the parking lot. Christine, the blonde in the group, seemed to be the friendliest to me. I asked for her phone number as I walked with her to a yellow Pinto. A couple of days later, I called the number she had given me and reached her at her parents' house where she was living while attending a local community college. After a brief greeting, she asked, "Have you heard of my dad? He's a judge." He was on the superior court in an adjoining county, but I didn't know of him.

"No," I replied. "I don't do much courtroom work."

She said, "Why don't you drive down to visit, and I'll introduce you? It will only take about an hour to get here."

On my first visit, I found out more about Christine. She was very outgoing, funny, and creative, always working on interior design projects. She had three sisters, and her father was a USC alumnus, former gymnastics champion, and district attorney of Tulare County. I thought he had a big ego to match his résumé. He seemed to want to be in charge of everything, and with four daughters, I thought he probably was.

I began making the hour's drive to visit Christine more often. After living alone for several years and being out on the town many nights, I found spending time with her family at their home comforting, and I looked forward to being there. During one visit she said, "Dad wants to take you swimming at the club. Would you go with him?"

This was another one of those "I should have spoken up" times. "Well, I'm not much of a swimmer," I said, but she assured me that was okay. Actually, after my near-drowning experience as a teenager in Rollin's Pond, I avoided swim parties and similar events.

"He's ready to go," Christine said, offering me a swimsuit. What I didn't yet know was that I didn't need a swimsuit as it was a men-only pool with no clothes allowed. I was not a fan of the water, and being naked didn't help any. Her dad kept saying, "Get undressed and come in; it's great!" I thought, *If he's trying to embarrass me and show who's in charge of this family, he's succeeding.*

Chris could see I was stressed about the situation. "Don't worry," she said. "He likes to show off sometimes."

Christine and I had many fun times in the coming months.

She was adventurous and was excited to go rafting with me in the huge rapids on the upper Kings River. We had to hang on to stay inside the raft while the guide maneuvered it with a single oar, the other having been splintered into pieces by the rocks. We went to the movies, rode bikes, played tennis, and shared many family meals at her parents' home. We began to discuss the possibility of marriage. Although I was older, neither of us had been married, and we both wanted a family someday. We continued to date for another year and then decided to marry. She wanted to have the ceremony on February 14, Valentine's Day, which I said was fine. Because I wasn't a Mormon, her family's religion, we couldn't marry in that church, so she chose a different location in her hometown.

We were married on Valentine's Day, and Mom and Dad flew out from Ohio to attend. Mom was not too pleased with my choice; although Christine was blonde and attractive with a bubbly personality, Mom thought the twelve-year age difference made Christine too young, didn't really like the Mormon idea, and saw her dad as a know-it-all. My groomsmen were my three brothers, all wearing light-tan tuxedos. Dale was especially glad I was settling down. "Ben," he said, "I'm really happy you're getting married and have decided to settle down. I was in the same situation myself. Though not as long as you, I stayed single and dated different gals, but finally it got old, and I wanted another life." I thought about the old black-and-white photo of Dale and two of his male friends along with three women, taken during his time in the Air Force. Dale, the tallest, was in the middle with a gal on each side of him and his arms around both of them. The other two guys seemed to be lost in the picture with Dale as the center of the gals' attention.

Christine and I flew to the Bahamas for our honeymoon on a remote island in a house that came complete with its own cook and maid. Two years after the wedding, our first son, Austin III, was born, named after both Dad and me. Four years later, we welcomed our second son, Brice. A number of years after that, unusual things started to happen. She began to leave our sons unattended, once in a hotel restaurant lounge, and other times I would need to pick them up on the curb at school after everyone else had gone home. She became distant and hard to talk to. She and a girlfriend started spending their afternoons drinking. Her family grew concerned about her behavior and took her for testing at a local behavioral health facility, which revealed a diagnosis of psychological issues.

Although our divorce was final in 1988, disputes over property matters continued for another eight or nine years with the never-ending parade of attorneys representing Christine. This was in the midst of my practicing law, working on developing a golf course, and taking care of our two sons, of whom the court had awarded me custody.

▶ THE SECOND TIME AROUND

In 1989, my sister-in-law Vonnie, Dan's wife, called me to ask how things were going and to express concern over my work and caring for the boys. She said she knew a nice gal who was single, had never married, and might just be someone I would like to meet. Shortly after that, Suzy Harris called me, mentioned my sister-in-law's conversation, and said she'd like to stop by my office. "Would that be okay?" she asked.

I said, "Sure, why not? How about this Wednesday afternoon about two o'clock?"

When Suzy arrived, my receptionist seated her in my conference room and let me know she was there. I walked in and introduced myself. She was strikingly good-looking, tall, and dark haired, and I still recall the long blue skirt she was wearing. We talked for a while, and before she left, I said, "Why don't we get together sometime?"

"That would be great," she replied.

The next time we spoke, she asked how I was getting along taking care of my sons. At the time, Mrs. Arlene White was helping me with the boys. Mrs. White's husband, a minister, had abandoned her and her son to live with another woman in France. Mrs. White had placed an ad in the local newspaper looking for work, and I had answered. She was kind and sweet, and the boys really liked her. I told Suzy about Mrs. White and said I'd like the two of them to meet.

I called Suzy and said, "Why don't you stop by tomorrow and help me get the boys ready for school, since Mrs. White won't be here until dinnertime."

She came by as agreed and in time to fix breakfast for the boys. The boys said, "I'm glad you're here. Can you just live here?"

"No," Suzy replied, "I can't do that, but I'll be around to take care of you."

Upon meting Suzy, Mrs. White said, "Oh, I'm so pleased you're going to help Ben." The boys and Mrs. White all liked Suzy.

Suzy and I saw each other almost every day after that. She began picking up the boys from school, helping with their home-work, and arranging birthday parties, soccer practice, and school events. She worked very hard at being their mother. On nights when Mrs. White was available to watch the boys, Suzy and I would go out to dinner or a movie. I started depending more and more on Suzy's help with the boys and her emotional strength amid the constant conflict with my ex-wife's attorneys. Suzy began to receive phone calls at my residence from my ex-wife's male friends, who would call her all kinds of names then hang up on her.

While Suzy and I started talking about being together for the long term, my thoughts returned to my concern about ever remarrying. I realized that I'd come a long way from the conflict of my first marriage, when I never thought I'd even consider marrying again. As the months went by, I felt more and more need to be together with someone. Eventually, I decided to buy an engagement ring and nervously went into a small jewelry store in downtown Fresno. I told the jeweler what I was doing, and I recall him saying, "Surely you will want something nice," a phrase I had heard before. Afterward, I called Suzy at her work and said, "I'd like to come by your apartment tonight. I've got something for you."

"Sure," she said. "What is it?"

I replied, "You'll see."

I put the ring in its box at the bottom of a paper grocery bag along with two champagne glasses and a bottle of not-so-expensive bubbly all wrapped up in newspapers. I opened the champagne and poured some for each of us. Suzy seldom drank, and this time only had a couple of sips. I said, "I think there's something else in the bag."

She found the box, and upon opening it said, "Oh, honey, it's beautiful."

In the coming months of 1991, Suzy and I discussed marriage plans. "Why don't we get married next year?" she suggested. "That way it will give us time to plan everything."

Dale and Glee frequently invited Suzy and me to dinner at their home. Oftentimes, Dale, who liked to cook, would make a big pot of spaghetti, along with salads and his favorite dessert, ice cream. During one of those dinners, Glee handed Suzy something and said, "Here, I want you to have this." It was a cup and saucer.

Suzy said, "Oh, thank you, it's so delicate."

Glee continued, "There's an old family tradition to give a cup and saucer to celebrate an engagement. I like old traditions, and engagements and marriage are the best."

The note accompanying the gift read, "A warm welcome to our family," and was signed, "Glee, Dale, Tiffany, and Dana."

Suzy and Tiffany always got along really well too. "She's so quiet and courteous," Suzy mentioned once. I thought, *The two are a lot alike.*

As our relationship progressed, there were numerous court hearings with Christine over the custody of our two boys. I didn't want Suzy to attend the hearings, as she was already helping me enough with the stress from my previous marriage. I also didn't want her to be called as a witness just for the purpose of embarrassing her. My former wife's attorney could call people seated in the courtroom to the witness stand without a subpoena. Even though she did not attend the hearings, when I arrived home from a long, stressful day in court, she always listened to me relate the events of the day and said, "This will turn out okay for you. I'm so proud of you and how strong you are to protect your sons."

I got along well with Suzy's family too. Her parents made me and my two sons feel welcome whenever we were together. In the spring of 1992, our wedding plans were halted when Dale, Glee, and Tiffany were killed. Before that, Dale and Glee had said more than once, "Ben, we are so happy you found Suzy. We really like her." Suzy and I were grateful to have had the time we did with them.

Finally, about five years after we first met, we set a wedding date of Saturday, May 21, 1994. By now the golf course I had been working on was complete, and Suzy really liked the idea of having the ceremony and reception there.

We gathered that sunny Saturday afternoon under the limbs of a large oak tree on the eighteenth fairway at Brighton Crest, as two families soon to be joined as one. My two sons and my brothers, Dan and Richard, were my groomsmen. Dad flew out from Ohio and looked sharp in his black tuxedo. Suzy's father drove a Lexus from their family auto dealership to pick up Dad at the golf course clubhouse, assuming he was more frail than he actually was. "Get in, Mr. Ewell," he said. "I'll drive you down the fairway to your seat."

Dad said, "That's okay, I can walk, but I'll go with you." They got along well except Dad thought my future father-in-law talked a little too much. I had so many good times with Suzy and her family at their home on holidays and special birthdays. This was a huge contrast with my previous in-laws, and about the only negative thing was that this father-in-law also liked to be in charge. Suzy's mother was a very pleasant, classy person with never a harsh word.

After the small ceremony, we had dinner with over two hundred guests under a large tent erected next to the course green, where we listened to a perfectly placed grand piano during dinner. A larger band played later, and their special "guest" that night was my twelve-year-old son, Brice, who played clarinet in his black tuxedo along with the band. Suzy leaned over during dinner and said, "Dale, Glee, and darling Tiffany would have loved this night." In contrast with my first honeymoon in the beautiful Bahamas, Suzy and I flew to New York on a business trip with my swollen hand bandaged from a nail puncture wound.

Four years later, the first of our three children, Harrison Dale, named after my brother, was born, followed by John Eli, whose middle name was my grandfather's, fifteen months later. Two years after that came Tucker Benjamin, called by Dad's mother's maiden name. Our three sons, along with the two from my first marriage, are the joy and love of my life. Still together after twenty-eight years of marriage, Suzy and I navigated the tragedy of family deaths, remnants of the continuing conflict from my first marriage, and raising our three sons while still attending to my two older boys.

Raising our three younger boys as an older father has been quite a learning experience. From a wooden crank telephone on the wall of our farmhouse to the age of cell phones, FaceTime, Facebook, Snapchat, YouTube, Instagram, TikTok, and all other social media platforms is a big leap. My Ohio-era temptation to drink 3.2 beer has been replaced by parents having to navigate vaping marijuana, opioids, and the deadlier substances like fentanyl and meth, so-called recreational drugs that pose an unbelievable challenge for today's parent, as I well know.

Chapter 8

DEATH
IN OHIO

An unexpected phone call from my sister, Betty, on the night of October 4, 1984, changed my life quickly and without warning. Betty lived in Ohio and had little or no use for California and its residents. Since she rarely called, I thought something must be wrong. Maybe Dad had had another heart attack or a broken leg like the time a cow kicked him, but it was not about Dad. Betty said Mom had suffered a heart attack at home that afternoon and been taken to the Elyria Memorial Hospital about twenty miles away. She had been watching a Major League Baseball playoff game between the San Diego Padres and Chicago Cubs on television with Dad. She'd felt severe chest pain but, according to Dad, chose to ignore it and continued watching the game for another twenty or thirty minutes before allowing Dad to call an ambulance. I called Dan and Richard with Betty's news, and the three of us ended up on a night flight to Cleveland later that evening. I spoke to Dale, and he said, "Ben, I'll fly to Ohio tomorrow and meet you there. I appreciate your taking charge of things."

To hear Dale, my oldest brother, thanking me meant a lot.

Richard said to me, "Ben, you look really tired," as we boarded the plane for our flight to Cleveland.

I replied, "I think it's my worries about Mom."

After a sleepless, all-night flight, we arrived at Cleveland Hopkins Airport early the next morning. We rented a car at the airport and drove to Dad's house about an hour west of Cleveland. When we got there, Dad was quiet and didn't say much besides, "Ben, I'm worried about your mother. I wish she had let me call for an ambulance sooner, but you know how stubborn she can be."

This wasn't the time to make a wisecrack. I just replied, "I know," and decided to go the hospital to check on Mom. Richard, Dad, and I drove the rental car to the hospital. Dan stayed at Dad's, saying he wanted to get some sleep and would drive Dad's truck to the hospital later that morning. Arriving at the Elyria hospital, I recalled Mom and Dad telling me later in life this was the place I was born, but I had never returned there until this day.

Mom was hooked up to an IV with some kind of liquid drip in her arm and a blood pressure gauge on her other arm. A tangle of wires and tubes were hooked to a monitor that beeped constantly. The doctor said we could stay only a couple of minutes and then we were to step outside so they could perform some tests. I leaned down through all of the medical tubes and wires next to her face. She didn't speak or move, but I thought I saw a faint smile on Mom's face.

When the doctor came back into her room, Dad, Richard, and I went downstairs to the cafeteria, and Dad ordered a cup of coffee. A few minutes later, a voice came over the hospital loudspeaker announcing that the cardiac unit nurses needed to return immediately, followed by the announcement of a code level alert. We didn't know what the code alert level meant, but it sounded serious, and I wondered if it was Mom they had been called to help?

Dad left his unfinished cup of coffee, and we hurried to the elevator and rode to the second floor of the hospital. As the elevator doors opened to the second floor, the window to Mom's cardiac unit room was directly across from us. I could see three or four nurses standing around Mom's hospital bed. As we walked toward her room, a nurse stepped through the door and stopped us.

"I'm sorry, you can't go in now," she said, motioning for us to wait down the hall. I could feel the tension and stiffness in my body as the three of us sat on benches lined up against the wall.

After we'd waited about a half hour, a white-coated individual approached and introduced himself as Mom's attending doctor. As we stood up to greet him, I had a strange premonition about what he was going to say.

He simply said, "I'm sorry, she's gone. Wait here a few minutes, and then you can see her."

I didn't ask what happened or how she died. I couldn't collect my thoughts enough to speak. Memories ran through my head like little pictures of Mom and my childhood. I could envision Sunday afternoon on the farm, Mom playing the organ at the Brighton Congregational Church and the piano at home as we gathered around to sing her favorite hymn, "In the Garden." Watching Mom graduate from college while I was still in school myself. I thought of the hundreds of books stacked throughout our house that she constantly read, only to collect more.

Richard bowed his head, either in thought or in prayer, or maybe both, and Dad stood motionless. When the doctor returned, he motioned for us to enter Mom's room. The window coverings were now drawn, and the space dimly lit and hushed, with the beeping equipment disconnected. Mom lay on the same bed where minutes earlier she seemed to faintly smile at me; her eyelids were now closed, her face pale white, peaceful, quiet . . . and gone.

Richard and I stayed for a few minutes. Standing by her bed, I bent down near her face and softly said, "Mom, I miss you. I love you," and then stepped outside after Dad said he wanted to stay a little longer and would be out in a few minutes.

As Richard and I started to leave the room, a nurse handed me a brown paper lunch bag. "Here," she said, "these are yours to keep." Mom's eyeglasses, a small purse, and some scraps of paper were inside. When we were almost out the door, the nurse added, "We couldn't get her wedding ring off." Playing basketball in high school, Mom had broken her ring finger, and after marrying Dad at seventeen, she never took off her wedding ring. Her finger joints swelled over the years from her injury, making the ring impossible to remove. I suppose it could have been cut off, but that's not something she would ever have considered.

Our concern now was Dad. After fifty-six years of marriage, how would he get along without Mom? Sure, they had bickered constantly over the years with plenty of comments from Dad about Mom's spending too much and from Mom about Dad not having done something to her satisfaction. Fifty-six years together was a long time, and neither had dated anyone else. One day when I was with Dad and upset, I said something negative about Mom. Dad immediately replied, "Don't ever talk that way about your mother." When he spoke to me in that way, I could feel the bond between them that had evolved over a half century.

When Dad emerged from Mom's room, he said he wanted to go to the First Wellington Bank and check a safe-deposit box he and Mom had rented in their name. The three of us said very little during the thirty-minute ride.

When Dad entered the bank that day, the teller asked, "How's Mary?" Dad didn't mention that Mom had just died; he just ignored the question and went to the safe-deposit box while Richard and I waited in the lobby. Dad returned from the vault without anything in his hands. He didn't say what he had been looking for, and Richard and I didn't ask him.

After leaving the bank, we drove to Dad's house, arriving about the same time as my sister, Betty, who had driven from her job at Ashland University. We called my brother Dale and told him about Mom's passing. He told us he and Glee would be arriving on a commercial flight from California the next day and gave the arrival time, adding, "Don't worry about picking us up. We'll just rent a car and get a room at the Oberlin Inn. You should go ahead and work out the funeral details." Dale, the oldest son, always had a good relationship with Mom just like he did with Dad. We usually looked to Dale for guidance on matters, but this time he was on his way from California, and we would need to begin without him.

Dan used Dad's phone to call the Norton Funeral Home. Dan, Richard, and I then drove back to Wellington later that day to meet Bill Norton, the owner of the funeral home bearing his family name. The facility was a large, stately, redbrick home built years before by one of the area's wealthy pioneers. It was set back from the street on a still, green carpet of grass with a large front porch, white pillars, and white gingerbread trim. The Norton family lived upstairs on the second floor and kept the caskets and held funeral services on the first floor. They did the embalming work in their basement.

Norton was tall, erect, and dark haired, with a slight black mustache, looking exactly how I thought a funeral director should. He knew Dad from being in the local Kiwanis club together. We discussed the details for the funeral, and he proceeded to show us the various choices and prices on caskets.

"You, of course, will want something very nice for Mary," he reminded us. *What were we supposed to say?* I thought cynically. *Sure, we want something nice.* It was clear to me that nice was related directly to cost.

He seemed like the character Digger O'Dell, the friendly undertaker on the old-time radio program.

We settled on a very nice rose-colored casket with a fluffy white satin lining and pillow and never raised an issue about cost.

I didn't know it then, but eight years later and another two years after that, I would repeat the casket selection process under even more traumatic circumstances.

On the day of the funeral, Dad, Dale, Betty, Richard, Dan, and I drove to nearby Wellington for the funeral service held at the Norton Funeral Home. We asked the pastor of the Brighton Congregational Church to speak at the funeral. Before it began, I went over to the minister and said, "I want you to say something special." He nodded in agreement. I continued, "She worked so hard raising us, found time to graduate from college and . . ." My voice drifted off as the organ started to play, and I knew the service was starting. We had asked beforehand to have some of Mom's favorite songs played at the service. With the first notes of "In the Garden," I thought of all the mornings I had wakened to Mom's playing that song on the piano.

It was a beautiful autumn day in October when we gathered at the little Brighton Cemetery under the maple tree with its bright red leaves. The grave in the cemetery's first row of monuments had a temporary marker reading, "Mary Rebecca Ewell, 12/30/1910–10/5/1984." Over the next few days, my brothers and I met with the monument company in nearby Ashland to select a permanent headstone. We chose a large rose-colored marble stone and asked the company to engrave it with both Mom's and Dad's names and to leave space for Dad's date of death to be added later. After Mom's funeral, Dad would go back to his home in Brighton with his pond full of mallard ducks and his rosebushes and live alone. We tried to hire a housekeeper or someone to cook for him, but he would not agree.

"I don't want someone standing around all day watching me," he said. Betty did go to see and help him almost every weekend.

I flew back to California and to work, and Dad flew out to California a few days later with Dan to stay with us. I thought keeping busy at the law office and my development project would help with my grief over Mom's death, but even being back at work, certain things set off my emotions. The sound of a particular song on the radio made me think of Mom, and my eyes would start to water.

▶ ANOTHER PHONE CALL

Ten years after our family gathered that October morning at the little Brighton Cemetery to bury Mom, another unexpected call from Ohio brought me face-to-face again with tragedy. Dad's neighbor Carl Farago called Dan to tell him that Dad's house had caught on fire. Dad had suffered burns and been taken to Cleveland Metro Hospital. When Dan told me the news, I drove right over to his house, which was not far from mine. He came out to greet me in his driveway. "What happened?" I asked Dan.

"I'm not sure," he replied. "I only have the little bit of information that Carl gave me. Carl said there was an explosion and fire at Dad's house."

I thought, *How could that have happened?* This time I called Betty. "There's a problem at Dad's house," I told her. "There was a fire, and Dad's been taken to the Cleveland Metro Hospital." I told Betty that Richard and I would be flying that night to Ohio. She replied, "I'll go over and check on the house and talk to Carl." I made airline reservations, and Richard and I flew together to Ohio that night to be with Dad.

As soon as we arrived at the Cleveland airport, we rented a car and drove to the hospital. We were directed to the intensive care burn unit on the fourth floor. This area of the hospital was very cold and stark with colorless, gray walls. Since the nurse said there could be only one person at a time in Dad's room, I told Richard, "I'll go first and then come out to let you know the situation."

The heavy gray steel doors in the hall in front of me had a small glass window at the top to see into the next room and a button on the wall that automatically opened the doors. I pushed the button with my latex-gloved right hand that was stained yellow and smelling of the iodine soap the nurse required me to apply before going any farther. To move from one room to the next, the steel doors behind you would close before you could open the next set of doors. It felt less like a hospital and more like a ship where sailors lock the hatches behind them before they can proceed to the next room. The receptionist had mentioned to me that the burn unit was very large and busy and treated patients of industrial accidents and burns from the entire Ohio Great Lakes area.

As I neared the last steel door, I felt the dampness of my palms and armpits as I began to sweat, and my stomach tightened. Seeing Dad was something I needed to do, something I wanted to do, but something I didn't know if I could do.

As I walked through the last set of steel doors of the burn unit, the smell of iodine became stronger, and I sensed something else, like the smell of fresh soil from our garden. In addition, I could now hear strange beeping sounds going off with different tones at different times, creating an electronic digital symphony.

At the doorway to the room the receptionist said was Dad's, a tall, white-haired, distinguished-looking man in a white coat approached me. He introduced himself, but I was nervous and didn't understand his last name except it sounded Italian, something like Dr. Castiglione. He motioned me over to a small bench to sit down. "You need to be prepared for what you are going to see today. Are you?" he asked.

I said, "Yes," very softly. I was lying; I knew I wasn't prepared.

"You won't recognize your dad." He then started to talk in a very matter-of-fact way. "You see, in very severe burn cases like this, we have a formula to determine whether the patient can survive. We factor in the age and degree of burn and have determined your dad has only a five percent chance to live. All the outer layer of his skin was burned and has been removed, and all his hair is gone. He is breathing only with the help of a ventilator that moves the air in and out of his lungs. We don't know whether he can hear or see anything since he doesn't respond. It's okay now for you to enter the room. Keep your mask on at all times," he added as he rose to walk away.

Even the doctor's warning didn't prepare me for what I saw as I stepped into a large hospital room occupied only by Dad. A gentle man whose favorite things in life besides his family were his rosebushes and the mallard ducks on his pond, Dad was in a place he shouldn't be. Dad's whole body was swollen, and the raw skin was visible with the outer layer gone. His head and face were bright red with an unnatural look. He was so different that, without being told his room number, I would not have recognized him. His swollen head was large and round like a basketball. If this were a stranger, I would have turned away to avoid the hideous sight. But this was my dad, and I was able to look at him as my dad and see past the disfigurement.

"Dad, it's me, Ben. I'm here with you," I said more than once.

He never moved his lips or even his eyes. He had not spoken since the explosion and fire at his house two days before. The investigators from the Oberlin Fire Department who had replied to the original emergency call believed the fire and explosion may have started when fumes from a small Briggs & Stratton gasoline engine ignited. The engine, hooked to a sump pump in Dad's basement, had caught fire and exploded. Dad, like many surrounding neighbors, kept a pump in the basement to remove water seeping through and under the foundation. The fire investigators thought Dad may have been trying to pour gasoline from a can into the small engine's gas tank when the gas fumes were ignited by the pilot light from the nearby water heater. For some unexplained reason, the explosion had set off the security alarm that Dad had never activated because he didn't want to spend the extra money. Hearing the sound of the alarm and the explosion, Dad's neighbor Carl ran to Dad's house, which was filled with smoke and flames coming from the basement. Carl said it was almost impossible for him to see. He said he crawled on his hands and knees down the steps to the basement. There he found Dad on fire, having been blown across the room by the explosion. Carl was able to drag Dad up the stairs to the front yard and lay him on the grass, wrapping him in towels and blankets he'd found in the house to make sure the fire was out on Dad's body. The emergency personnel wanted to transport Dad to Cleveland by helicopter, but because of a severe tornado-like storm in the area that night, he had to be taken by ambulance.

He seemed so alone in the hospital bed that day. I thought of all the times over the years when he had helped and encouraged me and was always there for me. How he had told me so many times to not worry about things that happen in life. I still worried then, and I worried now. I wanted to talk to him just one more time and hear more of his thoughts and advice. I told him, "Richard and I flew from California to be with you," even though he didn't respond. "Dad," I said, "I just keep thinking about all the times you helped me." He never blinked or moved his eyes or lips.

I saw him two more times that summer as I flew back and forth from California to spend time with him at the hospital. Shortly after my return to California from the last of those trips, a Cleveland Metro Hospital nurse called me at my Fresno office. She said they planned on turning off the fluids to Dad's body, and he would survive at most forty-eight hours. I can still hear her say, "The doctor is planning to go on vacation and wants to deal with your dad before he leaves." I couldn't believe what I had just heard. I asked myself, *Would Dad die now at this particular chosen time because of someone's vacation schedule?*

Someone must have agreed to have the fluids to his body stopped. I didn't ask, but my brother Dan said later, "It was probably Betty. You know," he continued, "she was driving every day to Cleveland, and the doctor had already said he wouldn't survive." Dan, Richard, and I never knew for sure who had agreed to stop the fluids, and we never asked.

I immediately scheduled a flight to Cleveland and returned with my new wife, Suzy. While we waited for our connecting flight in the Dallas airport, I found a pay phone and called the hospital. The night nurse on the intensive care floor answered my question before I could ask about Dad. "Yes, your dad is still with us, but you need to hurry."

When my wife and I boarded our flight to Cleveland, I didn't want to talk to anyone and waved off the stewardess who wanted to pass out sodas and snacks. I could only motion to my wife to get some water. I just couldn't stop thinking about Dad, and I choked up and got teary-eyed whenever I tried to speak.

Arriving at the airport at about midnight, I left the plane and ran to again find a pay phone, called the hospital, and asked to be connected to the intensive care burn unit.

I had barely said my name when the same night nurse I'd last spoken to from Dallas said, "I'm sorry, he's gone. Would you like me to keep him in the room until you get here?"

"No," I whispered, "that won't be necessary." I wanted to remember Dad as he had always been, with a laugh or a joke for everyone who could hear him. I didn't want to see him dead, swollen, and motionless on a hospital gurney as I had with Mom.

I mumbled on the phone to the nurse, "What happens now?"

She replied, "They'll take your dad's body to the county morgue tonight, where an autopsy will be performed early tomorrow morning." The thought of Dad being cut open with his organs and brain removed from his body went through my mind.

"Do they have to do that?" I asked the nurse.

"Yes, it's the law," she replied. "In a case of death from fire and explosion, it has to be done. You could call Mrs. Reynolds, the county coroner, in the morning, and ask her about the process, but you better hurry because they start autopsies at about five. Do you have something to write on?" I mumbled yes, and she gave me the number for the morgue.

I left the hospital, and we drove the rental car to my sister's home in Ashland, but I slept only a little, having set the alarm to wake up at four thirty so I could call the coroner before five o'clock.

I awoke with a start and used Betty's home phone to call the Cuyahoga County morgue. "Hello, can I help you?" the person answering the phone said. I explained I was the son of Austin Ewell who had died earlier that Sunday at the Cleveland Metro Hospital. I had been told that his body had been taken to this morgue.

"Wait just a moment," the gal on the phone said. "I'll check our records." After a brief time, she said, "Yes, he's here and sched-uled for an autopsy procedure shortly." I asked if I could speak to someone about the autopsy.

After the Cuyahoga County coroner got on the phone and introduced herself, I said, "I'm Austin Jr., son of Austin Ewell. We know he died last night from a fire. Why do you have to do an autopsy and disfigure his body even more? He's almost eighty-seven years old. He led a peaceful life and now has died a violent death. Can you please not to do this?" There was desperation in my voice.

"Well, it's the law in Ohio when there is a violent death," she replied. "We don't really have a choice."

There was a long silence on the phone, and then the coroner came back on the line.

"Well, I shouldn't do this, but I'll honor your request and forgo the autopsy," she replied. "I'll just sign the death certificate myself."

Over the next couple of days, Dan and Richard and their families arrived in Ohio, but this time Dale was missing. Once again Dan, Richard, and I met at the Norton Funeral Home and went through the casket selection process. There was no talk this time of choosing something nice; we simply asked Norton, who had known Dad personally, to make the casket selection himself. We decided to hold the funeral at the Brighton Congregational Church, with a public viewing at the funeral home the night before. Wellington was a small town, but several hundred folks came to the funeral home that night to pay their respects to Dad. In a gesture I greatly appreciated and could barely believe, my secretary, Toni, and Jay, the foreign investor representative in my Fresno project, flew from California to Ohio without my knowing to attend Dad's funeral service.

That ended my life with Dad. I thought about how hard he worked on our farm day and night, rain or shine. He knew something about everything, even though his education ended with high school. I thought about his humor, his laugh, the twinkle in his eye, and his sound advice. I thought about his love for his family, his rosebushes and the mallard ducks on the little pond next to his home. He was a man who, as remembered in an article by the local Ohio newspaper at the time of his death, was said to be "in this world, but not of this world." With help from his grandchildren, his casket was carried down the aisle of the Brighton Congregational Church where Mom had played the organ for so many years. We buried Dad at the Brighton Cemetery next to Mom's final resting place under the limbs of the same sugar maple tree. Their graves were located on the opposite side of the cemetery from Dad's parents, brothers, and sister; they remained separated in death. On the front of a large rose-colored marble stone installed after Mom's death were inscribed the words, "Together 56 Years and Now Forever."

Chapter 9

A NEW
TOWN

E arly in 1989, I received a call at my law office from San Francisco architect and planner Kevin Johnson. I had hired Johnson to design a Fresno-area development project I was working on, and now I needed his help to find investors for the project.

"There's a Chinese-Filipino group looking at a project in Florida," he said. "After that, they'll make a decision whether they are interested in your Fresno project."

Several years had gone by since I attended a Fresno County citizens' group meeting to discuss the idea of selecting a site for a new town. A key component in the update to the 1980 County General Plan called for development of a new town as a site for concentrated residential, commercial, and recreational development.

The county's idea for a new town in a rural area away from existing development was to offset increasing land division activity that allowed owners to split their property into smaller two-, five-, or ten-acre parcels. Dividing the property into individual small parcels had negative impacts on the surrounding land and residents. A house built on a small portion of a divided parcel usually left the rest of the parcel covered with weeds and junk. Problems on these small parcels became common where everyone had their own wells that often went dry and septic tanks that leaked into the groundwater.

After more planning and discussion, Fresno County was pursuing the new town idea but had not selected a location. The county was considering three locations for a new town, and one included property I owned in the foothills of the Sierra Nevada mountain range. This site was near the original town of Millerton, established in the late 1850s on the south bank of the San Joaquin River along the Stockton–Los Angeles road. At one time, Millerton had a courthouse, jail, tavern, and stores. It had served as the seat of Fresno County government until the late 1800s.

The original town had been named for Captain Miller, commander of US troops at the fort bearing his name. The soldiers at Fort Miller divided their time between keeping peace between the new settlers looking for gold and the local Indian tribes who had lived at that location for centuries. According to the story written about the fate of the original town, Millerton began in 1872 as Leland Stanford built his Central Pacific Railroad line south from Lathrop through the San Joaquin Valley with Los Angeles as its terminus. Stanford's crews laid train tracks across the flat, desolate Central Valley floodplain, and upon reaching the northern bank of the San Joaquin River, they stopped work until Stanford visited the area. It was in the heat of summer, but he saw lush green fields in the middle of a dry desert terrain. Apparently impressed, he directed that a stop on his railroad be built there, naming it "Fresno Station." It turned out that Stanford's view of the area in summer with irrigated green fields was the complete opposite of wintertime conditions at that location. Stanford's Fresno Station had been built in the lowest possible spot at the confluence of several creeks, resulting in consistent flooding. Now that a railroad and a station had been built, there was a move to make Stanford's Fresno Station the county seat. In 1874, the residents of the town of Millerton held an election and, as the story has been told over the years, the Millerton residents agreed, with help from whiskey handed out to prospective voters, to move the county seat to the Fresno Station site, which later grew to become the fifth-largest city in California.

The idea of starting a new town got me thinking of Brighton, Ohio. I liked to read about the history of how the first settlers in that area of Ohio had met in the 1800s to form their own new town, laying out roads and later building a store, school, and two churches. The formation and development of that Ohio area in the 1800s happened about the same time as the town of Millerton was thriving as the county seat of Fresno. Just as Stanford's Central Pacific Railroad line began to shape the Fresno area, the Wheeling and Lake Erie Railway or Nickel Plate Road had a big impact on the Ohio town of about five hundred inhabitants and the surrounding population.

I began promoting the land I owned as the preferred site for the county's proposed new town, and I came up against two wealthy, large landowners who wanted to have their own properties selected.

Knox Blasingame, who came from a pioneer family that owned thousands of acres of Fresno/Clovis–area land, wanted his site selected. Knox and his sister had several thousand acres to the south of my property and his brother Morgan several thousand acres to the east. Knox wanted to see the new town on other property he owned farther to the east at an existing historical site called Academy.

Knox, a likable guy, always played the part of the humble cattle rancher. He was shrewd, continually making money over the years selling or optioning pieces of his land to investors with big ideas. When their big ideas didn't work out, they ended up losing their money and land back to Knox after failing to keep up payments to him.

Jack Harris, another large landowner interested in having the town situated on his property, owned thousands of acres along the King's River east of the city of Fresno. I got to know Jack when I helped with political campaign events held at his home. In addition, he owned and farmed thousands of acres on the west side of California's San Joaquin Valley, maintaining what was said to be the largest cattle feeding operation in the United States with some hundred thousand animals. This was the epitome of industrial farming compared to the twenty-five cows we'd had on our Ohio farm.

As I rode with Jack in his green Rolls-Royce through the middle of his feedlot surrounded by thousands of cattle, manure flew in all directions from the wheels of his British luxury vehicle.

"This is a pretty nice car," I said.

"Nah, it's just a bucket of bolts," he replied. "It doesn't mean that much to me." He never took his eyes off the cattle trying to jump in front of us as he blew the car's horn.

I think Jack did feel that a Rolls-Royce never meant much to him. I've met others like him, and maybe this describes my own approach to life. Jack's desire was to accomplish things even if that meant going against the grain. I think that is what motivated him, not necessarily material things he gained along the way. I heard his friend describe Jack in a eulogy at his funeral years later, trying to capture Jack's essence: "The best way to describe Jack is he always wanted to buy when the rest of us wanted to sell." Sometimes in life, success or accomplishment of a goal takes place doing the opposite of what others tell you is the correct action to take. Jack successfully put this practice into action.

Over the years, I became friends with Jack's son John and his wife, Carole. They were well-known and liked and always active in politics and the community. I still have the photo of me standing in the winner's circle with John and our mutual friend Ward Kimble at the Bay Meadows San Francisco–area racetrack. After all of the years that have passed, I am now helping John with plans on the seven-thousand-acre River Ranch that his Dad wanted to develop.

As work continued on the new town site selection, I joined with neighboring Millerton-area landowner Norm Christensen, and began promoting both his and my properties as the site for the new town. I had first met Norm at his old ranch house adjacent to my property on a Saturday morning when he invited me to visit. Introducing myself, I said to him in a somewhat boasting manner, "I'm an attorney," thinking as soon as I said it that I shouldn't have.

Norm and I were as different as night and day but got along well most of the time. He could be tough and was afraid of no one. He liked to talk about the day he drove into the nearby Indian reservation, pointed his gun out the car window, and killed several of the tribal members' dogs that he suspected of chasing his cattle. No one else I knew then or now would have dared kill dogs on the reservation.

Norm, though a paraplegic, had no patience for people who claimed their own disability prevented them from doing something. He never talked or complained about his polio; he played golf, rode horses, went scuba diving, flew airplanes, and had very little use for folks who felt sorry for themselves.

As we worked together over the years, I learned a lot from Norm about the strategy of dealing with others, especially if they were your opponents. He would project an image of extremity, causing the opponent to be unsure just how wild he might get. Similar to my dad's name for observation of someone "off in the head," Norm would identify someone as "not having all four tires on the road." He was someone without a higher education but with plenty of street smarts. He and I didn't bother with written agreements, relying on handshakes and, more importantly, the need for each other.

I first became involved in owning land in the Millerton area by chance. Thinking of my years growing up in rural Ohio, I wanted to buy a small parcel of land in a rural area and started driving around the foothills at Millerton Lake outside of Fresno. I looked for "For Sale" signs but didn't find any. I did see a large hill across from the lake that caught my eye, and later I located the same property on the maps at the Fresno County Assessor's Office. I found the Southern California address for the listed owner, Tamera Investment Company, and I traveled to Los Angeles to meet with Nakor Tamera, the company president. He described to me his company's plans for their 1,500 acres (including the hill I first noticed) that they owned around Millerton Lake. He said they wanted to divide the land into dozens of twenty- and forty-acre parcels for use as weekend lake retreats, thinking folks from the Los Angeles area would want to get out of the city, park their recreational vehicles on the site, and stay there for the weekend. However, Tamera's effort to obtain land entitlements never got very far.

Then Tamera's son started coming to Fresno, thinking he might be able to do something more to move their project forward. As with his father, he didn't have much success with the project. I let both Tamera and his son know I wanted to buy some of their land but wasn't earning enough from my law practice income at the time to make any kind of a large payment. They kept saying they had no interest in selling but would keep me in mind.

After a year of silence, Tamera called me, and as soon as he began speaking, I sensed something was wrong.

"My family's been disgraced."

"What do you mean?" I asked. "What happened?"

"My son took his life. I cannot continue with the Millerton property," he added softly, explaining that in his Japanese culture, the suicide had brought shame on him and his family.

"You must buy all my property," he said.

"Well, I'd like to, but I just don't have that kind of money," I replied.

"You think about it; we'll find a way," he said, ending the conversation.

Thinking I should visit Norm Christensen to discuss what Tamera told me, I drove out to Norm's house and found he already knew what I had just learned. Norm already had in mind to buy the entire 1,500 acres.

Spreading out a map on his kitchen table, he pointed out the area he would purchase and the area he said I should buy, including the big hilltop I wanted.

"I don't have that kind of money; I can't buy all that," I told Norm. "How much does he want for a down payment?"

"Well, your share is a hundred thousand payable now," he said, and immediately added, "Don't worry, I'll make the payment for you and you can pay me back later." He never asked if I wanted his help. *Why did Norm do that for me?* I wondered.

The answer, I believe, as with most things in life, involved more than one reason. I'm sure in Norm's mind some amount of altruistic intention was coupled with gain for himself. The balance between the two motives can vary as much as the people involved with the giving. In Norm's case, I believe he did want to help me, viewing me like a son, and at the same time, he knew I could help navigate the regulatory minefields to move the development forward. He knew this was something he couldn't do on his own.

After Norm and I each bought a portion of Tamera's property, we began the process of moving forward with our future plans. Norm had heard about the county plan to select a new town site even before I did. He met with Lonnie Case, a young fellow from the nearby Sierra foothills who was serving as chairman of the county-appointed citizens' committee to study the new town idea. Lonnie was an unpolished character who got along very well with Norm.

While Norm worked with the foothills citizens' committee, I met with representatives of Fresno County to learn about their requirements for the new site selection. I was able to gain some insight into what the committee and the county wanted. I had spent a lot of time in local and state political campaigns after coming to Fresno and knew elected officials in a position to make decisions about the new town selection. I thought back to my Ohio road crew job and how politics helped me get it. This situation, while a different time and place, was really the same.

Jeff Roberts, a recent graduate of Fresno State University, had started a consulting business, and we hired him to help us with subdivision maps and planning at that time, something I knew nothing about. Norm and I became his first clients.

The hearing before the county board of supervisors to consider the new town plan was set for December 1984, about two years after the site belonging to Norm and me was considered for selection and just two months after Mom's death and the difficult time I was going through.

The board of supervisors hearing became a big deal with television cameras and a local newspaper reporter covering our project presentation. A couple of groups, concerned about protecting the environment, and Paul Bennett, a local radio station owner, stood up to oppose our project. Bennett, a well-spoken businessman with money, really got under Norm's skin. Norm leaned over at the hearing and said to me, "He just wants something for himself. He doesn't care about the environment."

Later, we found out more about Bennett. He and some others had the idea of splitting Fresno County in two and forming the new county of Ponderosa. This plan, if successful, would put our properties and the new town site just inside the boundary of their new county and under their jurisdiction.

A public relations battle started over the new county formation

with Norm and me both contributing money to defeat the proposal. Once again, with his direct, blunt manner, Norm gave TV
and radio interviews denouncing the motives of Bennett and the
other new county proponents.

Norm leaned over at the December hearing when Bennett
finished speaking and said to me, "Let me take him on. Just stay in
your seat."

Norm rose from his seat by pulling himself up and bracing
his arms against the seat. He steadied his polio-ravaged legs
and slowly moved forward, his crutches bearing his weight with
obvious difficulty. All eyes in the hearing room were on him as
he inched his way forward toward the podium at the front of the
room. His affliction was real, but he knew how to use it to gain
attention and sympathy. The hearing ended with a vote of four
to one with county supervisors in support. The lone opposing
vote was from a lawyer turned politician. He started his lengthy
discussion of our project by complimenting me and the project,
but when the vote came, he said no. I found more than once that
even when people start out with enthusiastic praise, they can turn
against you and not feel bad about their actions.

The new town designation was entirely on property Norm and I
owned. Dad had flown to California and was in the room at the
hearing. I thought about Dad's constant advice to never give up
and his success in changing the school attendance boundaries,
something others had said couldn't be done. I saw more clearly
how the persistence in life that Dad often spoke to me about was
the key to getting things done. "Ben," he said more than once,
"never give up on something you believe in and want to accomplish. Others, no matter how smart they are, will give up. You have
to keep going." Dad reminded me about Dale and how as a young
boy he used to carve the balsa wood airplanes that hung in his

room. "He always worked toward his goal to be a pilot," Dad said. "Something he never gave up on, and he succeeded."

▶ THE FOREIGN INVESTORS

With the land I owned now designated as the new town site, contracts in place for a water supply for the project, and Fresno County approvals, I just needed the money to fund the project. This was no small impediment to moving forward. I didn't have the fifteen or twenty million dollars we figured it would take for the initial development: the project infrastructure, streets, golf course, and residential lots. At this point, Norm, who had several other businesses in California and Oregon, decided to sell his land and not get involved in the development of the project.

After lengthy negotiations, I entered into an agreement with a Chinese-Filipino investment group recommended to me by Kevin Johnson, a San Francisco architect. The investors agreed to finance the construction and development of the project. They would pay me a salary and give me a share in future profits of the development company, which they controlled. The one condition of their proposal that concerned me was the requirement that my properties had to be transferred to a newly formed development company. Years earlier I had come up against the same requirement in the sale of the pistachio business I was involved in with my brother Dan, and that hadn't ended well.

The investment group's representative, Jay Levine, came to Fresno to meet with me. He said he would be living in Fresno to keep an eye on the project and, presumably, me as well. Jay was friendly, soft-spoken, an all-around pleasant person who never raised his voice or showed anger, and much smarter that he looked and acted. He held a master's degree from Columbia University and another from Fordham and was the author of several books on international trade and economics. During the next few years as I worked alongside him, I learned more about his culture and background and the caste-like system that he lived under in his native Philippines. His immediate boss would always be a superior to him, and the boss's motives and actions could never be questioned. This approach was unlike the modern-day American workforce and more like the Industrial Age. At one time, company towns and company stores were a necessary part of a worker's life. Workers didn't have the freedom they do now to advance and be their own boss someday.

The investment group began financing the project development at about the same time my divorce litigation became even more acrimonious with constant court hearings and depositions. My former wife's attorney kept filing various briefs with the court stating that they had a buyer for the project and that I had wrongly transferred to someone else the project's water rights I had previously obtained. This false statement made headlines in the local newspaper. It was corrected and confirmed in a public session of the county board of supervisors that, in fact, there had been no transfer, and it was Fresno County that held the water rights. Still, they seemed determined to either take over the New Town project or make it impossible for me to succeed.

In 1988, Jay and I, along with our staff, were working frantically to put together the document package needed for the approval of the project's first subdivision map, containing 420 residential lots and a golf course. The investors' Asian culture continued to influence our actions. They wanted the application documents filed on August 8, 1988, because eight was a lucky number. We managed to get the documents filed with Fresno County on that date, just barely making the deadline by hand-carrying everything to the county offices minutes before closing time.

Later, when we built the golf clubhouse, the Asian cultural influence arose again. Feng shui was used to determine the location of the entrance to our planned golf clubhouse. Jay had told me earlier, "Ben, we will use feng shui methods to place the clubhouse." He then tried to explain to me what this meant. After working with the clubhouse plans, Jay said the revised plans would satisfy the cultural influence requirement. I asked Jay why it was necessary. He said, "It's a combination of cultural influence and history." As an Ohio farm boy, we would consider construction placement as it related to storms in our area that usually came out of the west or northwest, but we never worried about choosing a direction and angle to allow the good spirits to enter the front door and the evil ones to leave out the back. Jay said sympathetically, "Ben, I can understand that you have trouble comprehending this cultural difference."

I replied, "Well, I appreciate that, and it's good for all of us to learn new things—and this is one of those times." The topic never came up again, and we each had respect for the other's perspective.

As work on the development started to move forward, our San Diego–based marketing consultants were struggling to find a name for the new project. Several suggestions included The Centennial Project and The Legacy, but there was no consensus among the group. The consultants and Jay were together in our conference room one afternoon trying to agree upon a project name. I walked in and told them I had an idea for a name. One of the consultants asked what it was. I said, "How about Brighton? It's the name of the little town in Ohio where I was born."

"You know, that might work," the consultant said. "That's a pretty good connection to the project."

We then decided to add the word "Crest" to reflect the hills on Christensen's property, where it would now be built.

The intended site for the project golf course on my property was still entangled in my divorce litigation and could not be used at that time. Christine's attorney had filed litigation that she had rights that had not been addressed and had filed a Chapter 11 bankruptcy, naming herself as owner of the property and entering into a contract to sell the project property to a party connected to her divorce. Later the court appointed an independent trustee to oversee the property. The investment group decided to purchase Norm Christensen's home ranch adjacent to my property to use as the golf course site. Now I faced a problem of credibility, having told the investors the golf course would go on my property with its mostly flat terrain. I had to convince them now that the course should go next door on Norm's property, which had a lot of hills, rocks, and rough terrain.

On a plain piece of copy paper, I had Jeff Roberts sketch out the golf course layout on Norm's property rather than mine, but of course the hills and steep terrain didn't appear on the flat piece of sketch paper. Reynaldo, Jay's boss, wanted to personally review and discuss the sketch of the new course location with me before approving it; however, he was at his home in London and wanted to meet there.

Boarding a plane the next day with the sketch in my suitcase, Jay and I flew to London and checked into the St. James Hotel. The morning after our arrival, a driver picked us up at the hotel and dropped us off at a London office building.

Gazing down at the sketch for about five minutes, Reynaldo looked up and abruptly said, "Fine, let's go ahead." Prior to his quick decision, I had mentioned to Reynaldo what Jay already knew, that the new site was hilly and not flat, but it didn't seem to bother him or change his thinking. He continued, "I think we should put a funicular on the side of the big hill."

After we left the meeting, I asked Jay what a funicular was. Jay replied, "It's a device like a cable car that is powered and climbs up and down on the side of a hill."

"Okay," I said, "but why here?"

Jay said, "They are quite common in other parts of the world, and I think Reynaldo had one that worked well in another project."

With the golf course location settled, we finished the course design layout.

Just four months after the August 1988 filing, the Brighton Crest subdivision map containing 420 residential lots and an eighteen-hole golf course received the unanimous vote of the county board of supervisors, and the project began moving forward. In addition to operating the development project, I still had a law office, adding to the turmoil in my personal life of raising my two young boys after the Fresno court awarded custody to me.

The investors started to demand information at all times of the day and night, often calling me at home at one or two in the morning. This may have been a good time for them in Asia or wherever they were calling from, but it was tough on me. I hung up on Reynaldo once at about one o'clock, and Jay Levine immediately called me back and said, "You can't do that in our culture." I wondered how long I could act beholden to this group.

We hired professional golfer and television announcer Johnny Miller to design the Brighton Crest Golf Course after Jay and I visited him at his home in Napa Valley. Following discussions and negotiations, Jay and I reached an agreement with Miller to design our course and help promote the development project.

Miller came to Fresno on several occasions to get ideas on fairway length and trajectory. Taking a set of clubs and a bucket of balls, he tromped around in the grass and weeds on Norm's ranch hitting shots from various angles. I knew very little about the game of golf, which had always seemed to me a waste of time spending hours knocking around a small ball. My obvious lack of knowledge also made me curious to find out more.

This was Miller's first California golf course design. He apparently didn't have a draftsman of his own yet and used some of Jack Nicklaus's team. Miller was friendly but had a somewhat sarcastic sense of humor. This personality trait came through in his later television golf announcing jobs. Other celebrity golfers I contacted wanted a large check for course design and use of their name, but Miller agreed to design and promote the Brighton Crest Golf Course and made the appearance at the grand opening in exchange for a number of Brighton Crest residential lots. At the direction of Miller, a Mormon, the lots were to be deeded to the Church of Jesus Christ of Latter-day Saints.

As the development project progressed, we needed to find a buyer for our finished residential lots. Our plan had always been to sell finished residential lots but not get into the homebuilding business. Even though we did not intend to build houses ourselves, we wanted a builder to create custom homes that would showcase and add value to the project. We found that most Fresno-area prospects were "flat land" builders who were uncertain about building on the hills of Brighton Crest.

I contacted a home builder, Lance Marino, from Danville, California. We thought he would be a good fit for the Brighton Crest project, as he had built expensive homes in Blackhawk, an East Bay high-end development with two golf courses and a large clubhouse. In the Blackhawk community, the grocery store came complete with a pianist playing on a baby grand piano in the entry and black shopping carts with gold trim. Lance promoted the idea of the "fully furnished" home. When owners of one of his Blackhawk homes arrived, they found a refrigerator stocked with food and chilled wine from an exclusive collection, a dog of their choice in the backyard, selected clothes in the closets, and dishes and silverware in the cupboards ready to be used. The owner's choice of music played on the sound system, and the homebuyer's favorite channels had been preselected on the television. Lance's unusual marketing style even caught the attention of the CBS's *60 Minutes*, which featured him on one of their Sunday night segments.

Lance's charm initially overshadowed his shrewdness, but when the real estate market went soft, he needed a way to get out of his contract obligation to buy every finished residential lot we produced. He filed a lawsuit against our development company alleging the lots he was obligated to buy were defective, along with a lis pendens notice, a claim recorded against the development property that stopped all our sales. With the recording of the lis pendens, we could not provide clear title to lots that were for sale. We eventually settled the suit and he was gone, leaving me with another reminder that things are not always what they seem.

A lawsuit filed against Fresno County by a group of neighbors calling themselves TEED OFF, which stood for Toward Enlightened Environmental Development Our Future Fresno, challenged the county's Brighton Crest project approval but didn't stop the project. If nothing else, I had to give these opponents to our project credit for their clever name. I explained the lawsuit brought by TEED OFF to Jay and the investor group. While by itself it was not a fatal blow to the project, Jay said, "Ben, I'm getting concerned about this litigation and your ex-wife's lawsuit and lawyers. The investors don't like to be involved in problems." The TEED OFF plaintiffs were represented by local attorney Richard Harriman, who alleged our project's groundwater wells would deplete the plaintiffs' nearby well water supplies. Now came the realization that, regardless of the favorable county votes for project approval, others could view all our hard work and effort completely differently. With their opposing motives and goals, I saw how they could put an end to everything I had worked so hard to accomplish. This same lesson carried over into my participation in politics, law practice, and relationships in life. Another one of Dad's admonitions from years before came to mind: "Don't worry about things you can't do anything about." While the saying that you should put yourself in the other person's shoes sounds good, it's very difficult in practice.

The TEED OFF case settled after a few months with an agreement on our part to restrict the amount of water that could be pumped from our wells, and it set a fixed time when we had to connect to a plant to treat the surface water we pumped from nearby Millerton Lake. The project area had only limited groundwater supplies and could never have supported a golf course and homes with well water without using the Millerton Lake water. We had always planned to build a treatment plant sometime in the future to supply the homes with drinkable lake water, but it would be expensive, and the lawsuit set detailed requirements and timelines for completing the plant. Now we no longer had the option to indefinitely delay the treatment plant construction and postpone the expense of the plant. The project issues were starting to pile up, and I constantly thought about the difficulty of living up to Dad's "never give up" motto.

To address the mounting issues, Reynaldo wanted me to fly to the Philippines to meet with the investor group. Jay and I landed in Manila at night and were scheduled to meet the investors early the next morning. Waking up in a hot, noisy, tropical city, Jay and I ate breakfast and were picked up by a driver who let us off at a downtown Manila office building. Jay and I waited about an hour in the office conference room before Reynaldo arrived, accompanied by two men, one elderly and one younger, along with a bodyguard. I learned later that bodyguards had become common in the country since kidnapping wealthy individuals gave criminals an easier way to make money than robbing banks or other more dangerous crimes. Reynaldo normally spoke to Jay and me about the project almost daily in perfect English. Now, he acted as if he barely knew who we were and didn't speak English at all. The father and son investors he brought with him sat quietly, appearing to be courteous and friendly. It seemed obvious that any problems or questions that day would be mine alone to handle. I felt that Reynaldo wanted to distance himself from the operations of the project. I asked Jay after the meeting why he acted this way. "Ben," Jay said, "it's his way of setting himself apart so if things don't go right, he won't be in the middle of any problem."

Reynaldo said the father and son were the primary project investors. He suggested I speak first and describe the Brighton Crest project. Through a translator, I gave a background on the history of Brighton Crest and what had been accomplished to date. They didn't ask any questions, and the meeting ended fairly soon after it started. After I finished my talk, they spoke in a Chinese-sounding language I couldn't understand.

Before we said goodbye, they mentioned wanting to come to the United States to see the project. The following summer, the father and son did visit Fresno. I reserved rooms for them at the Piccadilly Inn, but they were concerned about staying in a single-story hotel because they were worried about someone breaking into their ground-floor room, a concern that apparently stemmed from their homeland. They arrived about noon and suggested we have lunch at the golf course. The elderly man, Raymond, ordered a tuna fish sandwich at the clubhouse café. He reminded me of my dad and the Midwestern folks I had grown up around when he said to the waiter through a translator, "Just give me half a sandwich. I don't want to waste any food."

Maybe we had closed the cultural gap that day between East and West, at least the Asian East and my Midwest, as I could almost hear Dad saying the same thing if he had ordered the sandwich. This was a lesson I learned more than once, that when you think people are so different, you can find common ground, actions, and attitudes among us all. You just need to take time to look. Jay mentioned to me when the son visited Fresno that the son had no brothers and only sisters. The sisters in their culture would apparently have no role in the future family business. Jay said that someday the son would take over and be in sole charge of all of the family business investments. The problem was that at this time the son didn't seem to have much interest in the business. Maybe that was because he was still in his father's shadow when it came to this project. We can all relate to this situation and feel overshadowed by someone else, even if they are a family member. I experienced that myself when I was in business with my brother Dan. Although I thought I knew more than he did about a particular matter, I was reluctant to speak up or assert myself.

Reports of foreign investors being involved in the Brighton Crest project brought a lot of negative publicity. The United Press International headline read, "Former Marcos Official Involved in California Golf Course." Reynaldo had been a member of the former Philippine dictator's cabinet, and his deputy in the Marcos government was Jay. As it turned out, the author of that article had a connection to my former wife. This was followed by another article in the local newspaper about the Marcos connection. When the information came out, much of it unknown to me before that time, it made for spectacular media coverage, but the project and the millions invested in the project didn't change. Soon the publicity would die down. We didn't spend time trying to explain who the elderly father was. While the investor's money had not come from former Philippine dictator Marcos, trying to depict the investor, who had spent millions on the project, as the same guy who would only order half a tuna fish sandwich to prevent waste would be hard to accomplish. If I discussed the details, the privacy of the investor's involvement would be compromised, and it would become a never-ending newspaper story. No matter the facts, the article writer, as is often the case, would have his own agenda.

Doing business with people located on the other side of the globe with a fourteen-hour time difference required a lot of patience and planning. Dealing with two different cultures created a wall between us, something we never completely overcame. I had never done business with foreign nationals. Sure, I had visited numerous foreign lands, but conducting business with people of a different culture was different from meeting them in a restaurant or tour bus.

In addition, the never-ending lawsuits related to my divorce continued to threaten the success of the Brighton Crest development project and put the investors' money at risk. The investors' willingness to be patient with my situation was hard for me to understand. Could it be that suffering severe obstacles of their own in leaving behind their country and a collapsing government had given them a sympathetic side?

I think the answer involved some empathy for my situation as well as their need for me to help move along a project they had gotten into and couldn't complete on their own. Never quite sure of the reasons, I just kept moving forward on the project.

The rumors about the connection of Ferdinand Marcos to the Brighton Crest project brought out some strange behavior. The local Fresno FBI office called to say a woman had contacted them claiming the project developers, including me, had broken the law by bringing in tainted overseas money from the Philippines. I told Jay about the FBI call. He replied, "Don't worry, she might have the FBI, but I've got the CIA." There were other hints of Jay's ongoing role helping the United States. In the former Philippine government, he was known internationally and was responsible for dealings with Russia in oil and national resources.

What did he mean? I could only suspect from this incident and others that he had an ongoing connection to our government since leaving his Philippine government service, but I never knew for sure. The FBI agent later concluded the matter when he called and said, "Don't worry, we already checked out her claims, and there's nothing wrong."

Project coordination became more and more challenging. I had to oversee an office full of personnel, along with outside contractors, golf architects, engineers, county staff, and politicians. By itself, it became a full-time job, in addition to my continuing law practice and care of my sons.

Because most people I came into contact with at the course mistakenly assumed I played golf, I turned down numerous requests over the years to play, including invitations from visiting celebrities to Brighton Crest from the sports world. These included Michael Jordan of the Chicago Bulls after being selected MVP and winning the NBA championship and Steve Young after his Super Bowl victory as quarterback of the San Francisco 49ers. Both of these star athletes visited Fresno at different times, but for similar reasons. For Jordan, it was to hold a basketball camp for kids and to play golf. Through contacts in the Fresno State basketball community, he agreed to play golf at Brighton Crest.

Jordan had unbelievable stamina, playing thirty-six holes of golf without a break, and later that same night, he held a youth basketball camp session.

Jordan was personable, funny, and accommodating when I sat down with him in our clubhouse conference room and asked him to autograph fifteen or twenty items others had given me to get signed. They included basketballs, a baseball, pictures, and even a Bible. He didn't refuse, just asked me, "Man, where did you get all this stuff?"

Young came to Fresno and played golf at Brighton Crest as

part of his Forever Young charity fundraising efforts. His 49ers teammate Jerry Rice and the 49ers coach, who flew to Brighton Crest in a helicopter, accompanied Young.

Like Jordan, Steve Young was personable, friendly, and accommodating in signing footballs, photos, and other memorabilia. Both Young and Jordan treated my two boys really well. Both of these celebrity athletes were down-to-earth, as I learned when they were out of the spotlight. They have feelings and families and everyday issues to deal with just like everyone. We tend to assume celebrities are totally different, but except for their particular talent, they are not.

The disputes in my divorce finally began winding down with rulings from the court that appointed an independent trustee. He helped clear title to the property earlier purchased by the development company with investor funds. Over the period from 1988 to 1997, there had been ongoing problems and controversy surrounding the project, and the investment group started to hint about getting out of it. The constant litigation and need for cash to carry the project had drained them emotionally, even if not financially. The elderly father and his son who were the original investors reached an agreement to sell their interests to a Chinese-born fellow from the Seattle area. Patrick, the new owner, who had thick eyeglasses and a warm face and personality, discussed with me his ideas on the future handling of the project. This began a new round of relationships, issues, and cultural differences. The new investor's primary interest was in the golf course. He seemed to have little interest in the adjacent undeveloped New Town property I had transferred to the development company years before. He was involved in development projects in his home state of Washington and was a golf club member there. The golf course seemed to get his attention, but developing residential property did not.

Because of his lack of interest in the other properties, I began negotiations with him to see if I might buy them back.

Under the original investor group arrangement, the newly formed development company had taken over my land. My compensation as chief operating officer was supposed to be later augmented by development profits, which had never materialized.

The new investor had a different approach. He was willing to let me regain ownership of my original property and acquire additional land the development company had purchased from Norm. He told me more than once of his philosophical approach that I believe applies to many situations in my life: "There's no incentive for you to help me unless you can help yourself at the same time."

The first properties I bought back from the new investor were at a modest cost and a promise to pay most of the purchase price later.

Similar to the dealings with Norm years before, I believe both altruistic and business reasons entered into his treatment of me, and the end result was very favorable.

Real estate values began to fall in 1997, about the same time the new investor first arrived. By early 2004, when property values began to rise again and selling property at higher prices would be easier, another major project setback occurred. Our project relied on federal water rights from nearby Millerton Lake administered by the US Bureau of Reclamation. Years before, I had negotiated to obtain a source of water from water districts I knew from my work as a water lawyer. When I received an unusual after-hours call one night from Michael P. Jackson, the California Central Valley Manager of the US Bureau of Reclamation, I knew something must be wrong.

"Ben, get ready for some bad publicity," he warned.

"Why, what's going on?" I asked.

"A problem has developed over a line drawn on a Bureau of Reclamation map fifty years ago."

Mark Arax, writing for the *Los Angeles Times*, had published an article with the headline, "This Time, Developer May Not Get His Water." Michael said, "The writer had been in the Bureau of Reclamation's Fresno office, apparently looking through files and records, when he came across information that affected your project."

Since water being used for our Brighton Crest New Town project came from nearby Millerton Lake, a federal facility, the water had to be used in a federally designated place of use, an area delineated on a map many years before with a thick black crayon. The Bureau of Reclamation had mentioned to me years before some confusion on their part about the exact location of the boundary line for the federal municipal place of use.

They also kept saying over the years, "Don't worry about it."

Arax told me in a phone conversation, "You'll be glad someday that I investigated and found a problem with the location of the bureau's use line, because now the confusion can be resolved."

"Right now, I can't see the benefit of what you've done," I replied sarcastically. At least he was honest and mentioned that he had been contacted by my ex-wife about the issue.

No one really knew or cared fifty years ago about the location of the place of use line. Only when the black crayon of the 1950s drawing became digitized as a computer-generated map did they determine that most of our Brighton Crest New Town property appeared on the wrong side of the place of use line. The problem was eventually solved. After three years of regulatory and political maneuvering and resolving the objections from the twenty-two protestants to the petition filed to correct the boundary, the State of California changed the line, something others had mentioned could not be done, a reminder of Dad's school boundary success.

Later in 2007, the Chinese-born investor from the Seattle area wanted to sell his own interest in the project. I believe he had tired of the complexity and financial demands of a project in Fresno when he lived in upstate Washington and had his own real estate issues. Eventually, he agreed to sell back to me the Brighton Crest Golf Course and the rest of the New Town properties that he had acquired from the Filipino investors, who had originally obtained it from me. His terms called for fairly easy payments on a promissory note over a long period of time. After taking back ownership of the golf course and other properties, I borrowed money from a local bank and continued operating the golf course. While I was in the process of reacquiring the Brighton Crest Golf Course, I got a call from a Dan Castro, counsel for the nearby Table Mountain Indian tribe, saying they wanted to buy the golf course. After two years of negotiations, I sold it to the tribe and kept the rest of the New Town properties. Thirty years after first working with Norm Christensen and the citizens' committee, the overseas investors were gone, the project approvals were in place, all of the property was back in my ownership, and people began moving into the newly constructed houses.

A front-page article in the local newspaper titled "Foothill, Fate, and Faith" pretty well summed up the New Town project and my life during that time. The reporter wrote, "There were water problems, sewer problems, traffic problems, endangered species problems. There were money problems, up markets and down markets, failed partnerships with mysterious Asian investors, foreclosures, trustee sales, and lawsuits by the dozen. As if that were not enough, the past two decades have brought Ben Ewell enough personal turmoil to sink the strongest of souls. A vicious divorce that evolved into a decade of bankruptcy proceedings, the murder of his brother and two other family members and conviction of a fourth, and his father's death in a freakish flash fire. It has been a plague of almost biblical scale. . . ."

That article accurately captured decades of continuing effort on my part. Russell Clemmons, the reporter of the lengthy article, asked me the obvious question: "What if you had it to do all over again?" I hesitated, collecting my thoughts.

"I've given this a lot of thought over time. Do I get out or stay in and try to make something out of it? I decided to stay in," I told the reporter, and explained why. "It was my Ohio farm upbringing. My dad always said never to give up. He and my mother lived through the Great Depression. Growing up, we had no running water and no bathroom. I probably could have made more money with property somewhere else, but it wasn't just a business deal to me, it was a challenge."

After all of the years of work, lawsuits, and stress, I felt I had fulfilled Dad's advice to never give up. I have always tried to instill this same trait of perseverance and hard work in my own five sons as I have told them, "You don't need to be the smartest person; you just need to work the hardest."

EPILOGUE

Throughout my life's journey and this story, I have kept in mind several of Dad's lessons that helped me through both success and tragedy. "Don't worry about the other guy." "You don't have to be the smartest; just work the hardest." "Never try to show your superior knowledge around others who have very little of their own." "A smile or a laugh can do wonders." "Never let the other guy know everything you're thinking." And, of course, "Never give up."

I only wish my three younger sons from my marriage to Suzy could have had the opportunity to know my dad, their grandpa whom they never met, and learn from his humility and wisdom. I can't recreate the Ohio farm days I lived, but my boys love to hear the stories of those days during on our trips to Ohio and visits to the farm where we lived near the little crossroads of Brighton.

The two older boys whom I raised under a court custody order have grown to become wonderful men. I often recall something that the court-appointed counselor told me on a visit with my two sons: "Sometimes you need to close your eyes and take the thoughts in your mind to a place that's far away from the present, physically and temporally." In my mind, that place has always been the quiet, peaceful patch of woods at the back of my family's farm where in summer the thick canopy of leaves overhead made the light dim and the air cool. In my mind in this setting, I could take inventory of my life.

Even as my siblings and I diverged over the course of high school, college, and careers, it was always family that was most important—especially when tragedy struck. What kept me going through so much trauma was the family I still had left. Mom's death from a heart attack and Dad's death in a fire and explosion; Dale, Glee, and Tiffany's murder, which could never be explained or understood. This left a hole in me, and seeing Dad's tears upon learning his oldest son had been murdered by his own grandson will always be in my mind. Richard and I talk and get together often but without Dan, our always entertaining brother who died in October 2019 from Parkinson's disease. The sight of Dan's oldest son, Todd, carrying his dad, who then couldn't walk or move, expressed the cycle of life. Just as did Todd's naming his only child Tiffany, in memory of his murdered cousin from years before.

The years of publicity about the murders has caused me to be more private and protective of myself and my family. Like a new crop of blooms in the spring after the dead of winter, life does continue.

I have been married to Suzy for over twenty-eight years. Like any marriage, along with the happy times we have had, there have been other times that were not so happy. The three boys from our marriage are all getting ready to graduate from college as I write this. All the soccer games, baseball games, and sleepovers with their friends are in the past. They are all the loves of my life.

I think the tragedy in my life and the fact that I'm older than most dads has made me appreciate my boys even more. Harrison Dale will be graduating from Ole Miss and John Eli from the University of Arizona; Tucker Benjamin, our youngest, is attending Miami University, the alma mater of my three brothers and me. It was there that Dale joined the college flying club and began

ROTC training. This university has had a big impact on our family, and Tucker's attendance means a lot to me.

The younger boys especially like to hear the stories of Haight-Ashbury, and almost every time we visit our place in San Francisco, they go by 72 Central Avenue.

My oldest boy, Austin III, is a successful attorney heavily involved in water law as I once was. Brice, the second oldest, is licensed as a real estate broker and financial consultant. Austin III and Brice have each given me a beautiful granddaughter in Kaytn and Madelyn.

I still work nearly full-time in law and development matters on both my own projects and those of others. The New Town project continues with new owners who have purchased most of my holdings. While not the same as the farm in Ohio, but to keep interest in my rural background, I acquired a few thousand acres of ranch land that my three younger sons enjoy as much as or more than I do. Maybe it was just curiosity, but I checked to see about dividing up that land too. Under an agreement with local, state, and federal interests, I set up the "Austin and Mary Ewell Memorial Preserve," naming it after Mom and Dad, on seven hundred acres of the ranch property where others can now hike and enjoy the land and Finegold Creek that runs through it. I stayed involved in my community service projects and continue as president of the Fresno Police Activities League helping at-risk youths.

Writing this book has caused me to examine myself more closely, along with others. I always keep in mind Luke 12:27: "Consider the lilies, how they grow." Old photos have taken on new meaning as I look at my family through the years and appreciate our life experiences, both happy and sad. I've learned from the tragedies and the successes alike that we need to acknowledge the gifts of life, of others, and of the world around us.

I have had some success in law, business, politics, and community projects. In all of it, I have tried to create an opportunity out of every problem. I have tried to find humor and love for others and the world in which we live. I hope my commitment to never give up and keep going will be a useful example to others. I compare the days of life to riding a train traveling down the tracks toward the station. There are starts and stops, slow times and fast times. Along the way, some folks get on the train and some folks get off. The key is to keep going toward the station.

TIMELINE

OF EVENTS

To sum up what happened to some of the main participants in parts of this story, I wrote this list:

Dana James Ewell – Incarcerated for three consecutive life terms, without possibility of parole, in the Protective Housing Unit of California State Prison, Corcoran, California, as prisoner #P04759

1998–2012 – Appeals by Dana James Ewell to the Fifth District State Court – Denied

2004 – Petition for writ of certiorari to US Supreme Court – Denied

2006 – Filed writ of habeas corpus – Denied 2011

2012 – Appeal to US Court of Appeals for the Ninth Circuit – Denied August 1, 2012

Joel Patrick Radovcich – Incarcerated for three consecutive life terms, without possibility of parole, at Mule Creek State Prison, California

Sheriff Steve Magarian – Retired from Fresno County Sheriff's Office

Detective John Phillip Souza – Retired from Fresno County Sherriff's Office

District Attorney Ed Hunt – Deceased

Marvin Baxter – Retired from California Supreme Court

Michael Dowling – Executor and estate attorney, deceased
Ernest Kinney – Dana's defense attorney, deceased
Judge Frank J. Creede – Murder trial judge, deceased

Remains of the Victims – Dale, buried at Belmont Cemetery, Fresno, California.

Tiffany's ashes, placed on top of Dale's coffin. Glee's ashes were never found after Dana obtained them from the funeral home. The flat marker under the big trees reads, "Dale, Glee, and Tiffany, Together Forever."

Sherriff's Office Personnel – Detective Ernie Burke, Detective Chris Curtice, Allen Boudreau, Jack Duty, Detective Mindy Ybarra, Detective Stuart Huerta, Joe Flores, and many others – Always remembered for their hard work and dedication to solving the crime

Margaret Mims – Elected Sheriff of Fresno County

Ernest Jack Ponce – Now a California licensed lawyer, wrote a letter to the author dated January 10, 1999

". . . from the little bit I've learned about Dale, Glee, and Tiffany Ewell, I know that they were good, hardworking people, and they did not deserve what happened to them. I know I have a debt to pay to society for my part in their loss. I do not expect you to forgive me; I only want you to know that I am truly sorry for what I have done."

Monica Zent – A California licensed lawyer

John Zent – Retired from the FBI

Christine Ballantyne – Author's former wife. Wrote in a handwritten note to the author in April 2021, thirty-three years after their divorce

"I wanted you to know how grateful I am for all your hard work and efforts to provide for our sons. . . . I also want to apologize for the pain I have caused you. I'm sorry, please forgive me."

Mom – Died of a heart attack in 1984. Mom's brothers and sister, Lucille, are deceased.

Dad – Died as a result of injuries from a fire and explosion in his Ohio home in 1994. Fresno detectives held a suspicion of a possible connection to the Fresno murder case.

Dale and Glee's home – 5663 E. Park Circle Drive, vacant for eight years and finally sold at a fraction of its value after Mike Dowling gave the required California legal notice about the murders that took place there.

Norm Christensen – Deceased

James "Duke" Condren – Died in car crash

Dennis "Redhead" Searles – Successful and still active in financial and investment business. Resides in Santa Rosa.

Mark Arax – Successful author

George Baker – Retired from the newspaper business and currently a rare book seller

Bruce Murray – Living in Ohio on Aunt Lucille and Uncle Russell's farm at age ninety-three

Mary Jane Cavanaugh – Still editing PhD theses at age ninety-seven

Brother Richard A. Ewell – Living in Fresno and still trying to understand the tragedy of the deaths on Easter Sunday

Brother Rolland "Dan" Ewell – Died in 2019 of complications from Parkinson's disease

Big Glee and her two sisters, Grace and Helen – Deceased

Sister Dr. Betty Joan Whitted – Died unexpectedly in June 2009, the same day the author received her handwritten note she'd earlier mailed from Ohio that read, "May God bless you and keep you now and forever."

Suzy Harris and the author, Ben – Married in 1994, two years after the murder. In 1998, three months after the trial ended and the verdict was rendered, Suzy gave birth to the first of our three sons, Harrison Dale, then Johnathan Eli, and finally Tucker Benjamin, all currently attending college.

ACKNOWLEDGMENTS

For all those who helped me tell this story.

ABOUT
THE AUTHOR

Ben Ewell was born and raised on a small farm near Brighton, Ohio. He received his BA from Miami University in Oxford, Ohio, and his JD from UC Hastings College of Law in San Francisco, California. He practices law, specializing in water rights, in Fresno, California, where he resides with his wife, Suzanne. He is the father of five sons. He is also a developer whose projects include a New Town financed by foreign investors. Ben is active in his community, his church, and in politics, and he loves spending time with his family at his ranch in the Sierra Nevada foothills. This is his first book.

SELECTED TITLES FROM SPARKPRESS

SparkPress is an independent boutique publisher delivering high-quality, entertaining, and engaging content that enhances readers' lives, with a special focus on female-driven work.
www.gosparkpress.com

What They Didn't Burn: Uncovering My Father's Holocaust Secrets, Mel Laytner, $16.95, 9781684631032. What if you uncovered a cache of buried Nazi documents that revealed your father as a man very different than the one you knew—or thought you knew? In this poignant memoir, Mel Laytner, a former reporter, peels away layers of his father's stories to expose painful truths about surviving the Holocaust and its aftermath.

The Restless Hungarian: Modernism, Madness, and The American Dream, Tom Weidlinger. $16.95, 978-1-943006-96-0. A revolutionary, a genius, and a haunted man . . . The story of the architect-engineer Paul Weidlinger, whose colleagues called him "The Wizard," spans the rise of modern architecture, the Holocaust, and the Cold War. The revelation of hidden Jewish identity propels the author to trace his father's life and adventures across three continents.

Engineering a Life: A Memoir, Krishan K. Bedi. $16.95, 978-1-943006-43-4. A memoir of Krishan Bedi's experiences as a young Indian man in the South in the 1960s, this is a story of one man's perseverance and determination to create the life he'd always dreamed for himself and his family, despite his options seeming anything but limitless.

Social Media Isn't Social: Rediscovering the lost art of face-to-face communication, Al Maag. $15, 978-1940716459. With humor and insight born of decades of experience, Al Maag shares what he learned during his Chicago childhood in the 1950s and 60s, a stark contrast to the current C-generation that has grown up with electronic gadgets. *Social Media Isn't Social* shows why online social media cannot replace face-to-face human connection, and reveals the critical real-life social skills you need to succeed today in business and in life.

The Journalist: Life and Loss in America's Secret War, Jerry A. Rose and Lucy Rose Fischer, $16.95, 978-1-68463-065-3. A collaboration between Lucy Rose Fischer and her late brother, *The Journalist* tells the story of Jerry Rose, a young journalist and photographer who exposed the secret beginnings of America's Vietnam War in the early 1960s. He interviewed Vietnamese villagers, embedded himself with soldiers, and wrote the first major article about American troops fighting in Vietnam.